THE
AMERICAN CREED

OTHER BOOKS BY FORREST CHURCH

Father & Son

The Devil & Dr. Church

Entertaining Angels

The Seven Deadly Virtues

Everyday Miracles

A Chosen Faith
(with John A. Buehrens)

God and Other Famous Liberals

Life Lines

Lifecraft

Bringing God Home

Editor

Continuities and Discontinuities in Church History
(with Timothy George)

The Essential Tillich

The Macmillan Book of Earliest Christian Prayers
(with Terrence J. Mulry)

The Macmillan Book of Earliest Christian Hymns
(with Terrence J. Mulry)

The Macmillan Book of Earliest Christian Meditations
(with Terrence J. Mulry)

One Prayer at a Time
(with Terrence J. Mulry)

The Jefferson Bible

Without Apology: Selected Writings of A. Powell Davies

*Restoring Faith: America's Religious Leaders
Answer Terror with Hope*

THE
AMERICAN CREED

A Biography of the Declaration of Independence

FORREST CHURCH

St. Martin's Press ≈ New York

www.stmartins.com

Excerpt from *The Collected Poems of Langston Hughes* by Langston Hughes, copyright © 1994 by the Estate of Langston Hughes. Used by permission of Alfred A. Knopf, a division of Random House, Inc.

Excerpt from "An Ode to America," in *Evenimentul Zilei* by Cornel Nistorescu, September 24, 2001. Used by permission of Cornel Nistorescu.

The Library of Congress has cataloged the original edition as follows:

Church, F. Forrest.
    The American creed : a spiritual and patriotic primer / Forrest Church.—1st ed.
        ISBN 978-0-312-30344-0
        1. United States—Religion. 2. Religion and politics—United States.
I. Title

    BL2525.C49 2002
    200'.973—dc21

                                                    2002069832

                    ISBN 978-0-312-55505-4

        10   9   8   7   6   5   4   3   2   1

To my children,
Frank, Nina, Jacob, and Nathan,
with love and hope

I have often inquired of myself what great principle or idea it was that kept this Confederacy so long together. It was not the mere matter of separation of the colonies from the motherland, but that sentiment in the Declaration of Independence which gave liberty not alone to the people of this country, but hope to all the world, for all future time.

> —*Abraham Lincoln,*
> *Extemporaneous Address in Philadelphia,*
> *February 22, 1861*

CONTENTS

PREAMBLE

Wₕₑₙ ₜₕₑ ₒₒᵤₙₑᵣₛ WHEN THE FOUNDERS GATHERED ONE WILTINGLY HOT JULY IN Philadelphia to hammer out their dreams into a single, ringing declaration, they were fashioning precepts as sacred as they were secular. As a group, they were not notably religious men. But they were united, almost miraculously, in forging a union that transcended, even as it encompassed, the historical particularity of the present crisis. Fired with ardor and apprehension—the prospect of a long war, its outcome uncertain—America's first citizens performed an almost perfect act of alchemy. In their crucible were transfigured the elements that would reflect America's promise and set the measure for its fulfillment.

This new nation was, as the founders knew, an experiment. Like all experiments, it started with a precept, a "given"—in this case a set of truths so rock-ribbed and essential that they were deemed "self-evident." Truth cast in language that, in turn, spells out the truth for succeeding generations deserves to be called a creed. So it is with Thomas Jefferson's preamble to the

Declaration of Independence. The faith of a nation is captured in its words, words that distill a mission while investing future citizens with a sacred charge.

"Creed" sounds forbidding and ecclesiastical. The American Creed is neither, but it is monumental. Creeds have to be monumental, struck in metal that, when refined in the furnace of history and burnished by developing thought, can endure the trials of time. They have to be steadfast enough to redeem history itself, reawakening tired minds, rekindling passion in hearts grown weary. Creeds are spiritual touchstones. They are finished in fire, yet cool to the touch when passed from hand to hand one generation to the next.

Capturing the essence of the American experiment, the American Creed affirms those truths our founders held self-evident: justice for all, because we are all created equal; and, liberty for all, because we are all endowed by the Creator with certain inalienable rights. America's fidelity to this creed is judged by history. Living up to it remains a constant challenge. But it invests our nation with spiritual purpose and—if we honor its precepts—a moral destiny.

This book sketches the biography of the Declaration of Independence by charting the actions of those who most enduringly inspired, formulated, and embodied it. Readers will recognize most of them: Jonathan Edwards, George Washington, Abraham Lincoln, Eleanor Roosevelt, Martin Luther King, Jr. Others may be less familiar. Together, they illustrate the spiritual history of a nation.

Non-Americans may appreciate the nation's unique foundation more clearly than Americans themselves do. It was an English author, G. K. Chesterton, who first said, "America is the only nation in the world that is founded on a creed," one set forth "with theological lucidity in the Declaration of Independence." He memorably called America "a nation with the soul of a church." Though the American Creed as fashioned by Thomas Jefferson and perfected by the Continental Congress rests upon a clear separation between church and state, the body politic *does* have a soul. Chesterton assumed that the American

Creed condemned atheism, since it secures human rights as inalienable gifts from God. The saving irony is that this same creed
(as interpreted in the Bill of Rights) also protects atheists against
the coercion of believers.

Another foreign observer, Sweden's Gunnar Myrdal, recognized the self-correcting nature of what he too called "the American Creed." In schools, courts, and houses of worship, we teach
this creed to correct our nation's course as well as to celebrate
it. "America," Myrdal concludes, "is continuously struggling for
its soul." Pointing to the ongoing battle for civil rights, he recognized the tension between American ideals and their incomplete fulfillment. Yet, unlike much self-criticism—which can
easily lapse into self-loathing—the critique of this thoughtful
observer was charged with appreciation and hope. He read
American history as "the gradual realization of the American
Creed."

The nation's greatest leaders have viewed American history
in the same light. Abraham Lincoln saw the Declaration of Independence as "spiritually regenerative." The touchstone of
what he called "our ancient faith," its "sacred principles" establish the spiritual and political foundation for America. Inclusive
and chastening, the American Creed rings forth the good news
that all people are entitled to equal justice and invested with
equal dignity. Lincoln expresses this promise with almost unimaginable poignancy in his Gettysburg Address. Praying for the
rebirth of freedom, his language is biblical in cadence and theme.
It is also thoroughly American. Through the sacrifices of its citizens and at the time of its greatest trial, the nation could finally
attain its moral promise. A century later—forty years ago—
within sight of the memorials dedicated to Jefferson and Lincoln
in Washington, D.C., Martin Luther King, Jr., inspired a new
generation of American citizens when he said, "I have a dream
that one day this nation will rise up and live out the true meaning of its creed."

As understood by Lincoln, King, and many others, America
is a union of faith and freedom, in which faith elevates freedom
and freedom tempers faith. The American Creed doesn't impose

parochial faith upon its citizens but protects freedom, including freedom of religion, by invoking a more universal authority. Though employing the language of faith, it transcends religious particulars, uniting all citizens in a single covenant. It treats believer and atheist alike, offering each the same protections, securing freedom of and from religion. Equally important, it protects freedom from itself, tempering excesses of individual license by postulating a higher moral code. In America, faith and freedom wed to form a union greater than either alone is capable of sustaining.

Most Americans perceive no fundamental conflict between the practice of their individual religious beliefs and the latitude given to their neighbors to practice theirs. At our best, we celebrate both what sets us apart (specific doctrinal convictions) and what holds us together (a common faith). Some Americans— fundamentalists of the right and left—struggle more than the average citizen with such ambiguity. Respectively seeking to expand the compass of their piety or to remove every vestige of it from the public square, they shape the national debate both on church and state and on religion and politics. Negative images of each other, advocates for a Christian or a secularist vision of America alike misread the script of our founders.

Some call for a return to what they proclaim to be our founders' faith. They excoriate the nation for its loss of values, often persuasive in their critique but misguided in their understanding of the American way and of American history. Secularists on the left are equally wrongheaded. If ours is explicitly not a Christian nation, it is nonetheless built on a religious foundation. By law, church and state are separate in America, to the signal advantage of both. But by tradition, religion and politics are interdependent, especially at times of crisis.

As an ism, secularism suggests a rejection of or hostility toward religion. Taken in this sense, it dates from the French Revolution, not the American one. Reminding us of this distinction, years ago another clear-eyed visitor (a Dominican priest from France) made an observation so chilling and timely that I quote it here at length.

[Here] is where America missed the boat. It is because your country's spiritual dimension was not apparent to the peoples of the world that, ultimately, you did not win their hearts. When someone has lived right in the middle of the United States for eight years, as I did, he knows that spiritual dimension does exist; he knows to what extent the citizens and the collectivities of America are imbued with Christianity and a very original concept of individual dignity and political freedom. But this was not obvious outside the States. Your wealth and prodigality dazzled the world, but it did not seem as though you had any soul. That is what I so strongly hold against your great writers: they are read throughout the world, but they were not able, or willing, to tell the world what kind of heart and spirit you have. People concluded that you didn't have any. You were envied, but you were not loved.

Today, not being loved understates the reality. In many quarters of the world we are resented—even hated—for our perceived embrace of godless and value-free materialism and the felt imposition of this "decadence" on world society. To the extent that this characterization in fact represents today's America, we have lost our way.

To find the path homeward, we carry a map in our wallets. The very currency that facilitates our commerce reminds us that we trust not in the power of our wealth or might but in a power greater and more abiding. On the front of a one-dollar bill is the seal of the United States Treasury, its key pictured together with a carpenter's square for rectitude and scales for balance. On the back, flanking a portrait of George Washington, the father of our country, is the Great Seal of the United States. *Annuit coeptis*, the Great Seal reads: "[God] has favored our undertaking," and *Novus ordo seclorum*: "A new order of the ages [has commenced]." These mottoes are illustrated by a pyramid, bright with the eastern sun rising, dark on its western side, suggesting that the American experiment has just dawned. Drawn from Masonic symbolism familiar to the founders and expressive of Enlightenment religious values, this pyramid is uncapped, the foundation (crafted by human arts) completed transcendentally by a luminous, all-seeing eye, an ancient symbol for divinity.

On July 4, 1776, immediately after the Declaration of Independence was adopted, Congress entrusted Benjamin Franklin, Thomas Jefferson, and John Adams with the task of designing the Great Seal. Franklin later toyed with the motto "Mind Your Business," a double entendre that evoked the spirits of American commerce and American individualism. Here he and the others sought more transcendent symbolism. To the committee (as Adams reported to his wife, Abigail), Franklin proposed picturing "Moses lifting up his wand and dividing the Red Sea, and Pharaoh in his chariot overwhelmed with the waters." Adams himself suggested Hercules, under the motto "Rebellion to tyrants is obedience to God." Jefferson imagined the children of Israel in the wilderness on one side and Saxon chiefs, "whose political principles and form of government we have assumed," on the other. In each working concept, faith and freedom were joined.

According to the final design, on the obverse of the seal is an eagle, holding both arrows and an olive branch but looking toward the branch (an ancient symbol for peace). Arrayed above the eagle is a constellation of thirteen stars, representing the original thirteen states. In its beak waves a banner reading, *E pluribus unum* ("Out of many, one"), expressing the essence of our nation's creed. Linking these symbols and mottoes on our currency are the words "In God we trust."

Our currency is woven from a linen and cotton blend, fabric that can be torn only with difficulty. When we sever our trust in the high ideals on which the nation was founded, we tear something greater than our currency's face value and may rightly earn the world's scorn. Yet, when we rise to the challenge, we answer that scorn with a stronger love. We bear witness to a treasured set of principles that offer to a divided world the saving vision of our forebears.

Calling these ideals to mind—and directed especially to those who hold the future in their hands—*The American Creed* journeys through the highlights of American history, revisiting our national hymns, holidays, sacred texts, and shrines. I write not as a historian but as an American citizen and spiritual guide. My goal is not knowledge alone but meaning as well. I ask not only What exactly were our ancestors thinking when they said this or did that? but also What do their words and actions mean for us today?

George Santayana famously warned, "Those who cannot remember the past are condemned to repeat it." This statement suggests that the past is a record of error, which it is our business to correct. I believe that to be the truth but not the whole truth. When we forget our history—especially when we forget the principles on which our nation was founded—we also are doomed to fail to live up to it. We attack our own history as if we were investigative reporters, looking for the ugly truth behind its shining facade. By devoting so much energy to critiquing our past (a very American thing to do, by the way), we may, I fear, be losing an appreciation for the principles upon which America was established. Yes, our forebears often failed to live up to their ideals. That is partly because these ideals were so lofty. The greater our aspirations, the more certain it is that we will fail to live up to them. Such failure has its own nobility. Our ancestors set the bar high.

How the next generation answers the challenge posed by the American Creed matters enormously. At stake is not only the future of a nation but also—given America's power and promise—the future of the world. To live up to the promise of our creed, we must rekindle aspirations for its attainment. To such an end I offer this biography of the Declaration of Independence.

Equal and exact justice to all . . . of whatever state or persuasion, religious or political; peace, commerce, and honest friendship with all nations, entangling alliances with none. . . . Freedom of religion, freedom of the press, and freedom of person. . . . These principles form the bright constellation which has gone before us, and guided our steps through an age of revolution and reformation. The wisdom of our sages and the blood of our heroes have been devoted to their attainment. They should be the creed of our political faith, the text of civil instruction, the touchstone by which to try the services of those we trust; and should we wander from them in moments of error or alarm, let us hasten to retrace our steps and to regain the road which alone leads to peace, liberty, and safety.

—*Thomas Jefferson,*
First Inaugural Address

THE
AMERICAN CREED

1

"A City on a Hill"

"In the beginning all the world was America."

—*John Locke,*
Second Treatise on Government, 49, 1

In the beginning, when God created heaven and earth, all the world was a wilderness. This wilderness was populated first by ferns and then by animals. Hundreds of millions of years later, as a home to aboriginal peoples scattered in pockets around the globe, the world was a forbidding garden. Slowly, this garden was cultivated. With cultivation came civilization; city-states became nations; nations, empires. Where advanced civilizations flourished, nature was conquered and society tamed. But a new wilderness beckoned. The virgin American woods had their own story, an oral history passed down by Shamans of a hundred tribes. To European eyes, however, America was a second Eden. Long since driven from the garden, the first white settlers brought to America their own ancestral legends of creation and fall as contained in the Bible, together with a script for redemption.

The Pilgrims' and Puritans' migration to America was a self-conscious "errand into the wilderness," motivated by a hunger for religious freedom. "Behold I will do a new thing," God sang in the voice of Isaiah. "Now it shall spring forth; shall ye not know it? I will even make a way in the wilderness and rivers in the desert . . . to give drink to my people, my chosen." The Puritans thought that God was speaking through Isaiah directly to them. For better and for worse, the imprint this conviction left on our nation lingers to this day. Looking back on America's first New Englanders some two centuries after they landed in Plymouth Bay and Salem Harbor, Alexis de Tocqueville reminded us, "It must never be forgotten that religion gave birth to Anglo-American society. In the United States, religion is therefore mingled with all the habits of the nation and all the feelings of patriotism, whence it derives a peculiar force."

President William Howard Taft knew his history well. "We speak with great satisfaction of the fact that our ancestors—and I claim New England ancestry—came to this country in order to establish freedom of religion," he said in a speech celebrating the 250th anniversary of Norwich, Connecticut, in 1909. "Well, if you are going to be exact, they came to this country to establish freedom of their religion, and not the freedom of anybody else's religion." It is certainly true that when the Pilgrims arrived on the shores of New England they sought religious freedom from one established religion with the stated intention of establishing a new one. Yet the logic that informed their own liberation led directly, if unintentionally, to the establishment of freedom for others. Adam and Eve lost their freedom by exercising it. The Pilgrims and Puritans spread theirs by doing the same. It is no exaggeration to say that America's cornerstone is religious liberty.

From the very outset—even in documents that spring from a different set of primary intentions—one can trace the beginnings of what came to be established as the American Creed. From 1620 onward, faith has invested the freedom Americans seek with meaning. And freedom has tempered the exclusionary strictures of faith. We celebrate both of these legacies on Thanksgiving.

*   *   *

For most Americans the history we remember is associated with holidays. In pageants and ceremonial addresses our past is brought alive again. The teaching of our history begins here, in school auditoriums and houses of worship, at great outdoor festivals and colorful parades, and around the family table. One of our public national holidays, Christmas, is explicitly religious, a continuing reminder of the nation's Christian roots. The others are secular, each evoking shared pieties and therefore spiritual in a more distinctively American way. To know a nation's spirit, look first to its holidays.

In America we celebrate Labor Day, not Business Day. We remember those who sacrificed their lives for their country on Memorial Day and those who served to defend it on Veterans Day. Columbus Day marks the beginning of our country's recorded history, an occasion on which today we also reflect on sins committed against Native Americans consequent to America's "discovery." We commemorate the birthdays of two presidents, George Washington and Abraham Lincoln, ensuring that their stories and values will be remembered. On the Fourth of July we celebrate the Declaration of Independence. On the Martin Luther King, Jr., holiday we lift up a martyr's dream that one day its promise might be fulfilled. And on Thanksgiving—the quintessential American holiday—we look back to Plymouth Plantation. Thankful for family, the bounty of the earth, and our cherished freedoms, we join in prayer at the table of our first ancestors (Pilgrim and Native American alike). Thanksgiving is our most distinctive national holiday. According to opinion polls, it is also our favorite.

To serve the nation's higher interests, the celebration of our history must be instructed by fact as well as legend. Though they represent the most traveled bridge to our history, holidays can homogenize the past, making it less relevant to the present and instructive for the future. Thanksgiving itself is a perfect example. When William Bradford led his tiny band of Pilgrims on a perilous voyage across the ocean to a new land, the entire enterprise represented an act of faith. By the end of the first winter, half the party of some one hundred men, women, and children was dead. Starvation was commonplace, disease rampant. The Pilgrims and Indians coexisted in a tenuous state of justifiably mutual mistrust. That the Pilgrims could devote their attention to anything beyond sheer survival is almost a miracle. Yet, judging from the earliest records, their minds remained fixed on two things above all others: God and freedom.

Thanksgiving, our most religious non-Christian holiday, symbolizes everything that unites us as Americans. No one is excluded from its table of communion. In a sense, Thanksgiving is an American seder. Not only does a Passover seder's meal-centered and family-driven focus evoke the spirit of the Thanksgiving feast, but the ancient Hebrews' forty-year passage through the wilderness to freedom (which Passover commemorates) was the scriptural model for the Pilgrims' own journey to America.

Were we to open our Thanksgiving liturgy with a unison reading of the first sacred text of American history, it would begin with the words, "In the name of God. Amen." What the Mayflower Compact goes on to say is really quite amazing. A newly free people, after giving lip service to their loyalty to the "dread Sovereign Lord King James," did something on their own for which no other group in England would have mustered the gumption. They determined "solemnly and mutually, in the presence of God and one another, [to] covenant and combine ourselves together into a civil body politic, for our better ordering and preservation." In short, they created their own government, pledging to "enact, constitute, and frame such just and equal laws, ordinances, acts, constitutions, and offices, from time to time, as shall be thought most meet and convenient for the general good of the Colony: unto which we promise all due submission and obedience." Noting the contrast between this compact and the laws of the old country, Tocqueville exclaimed in wonder, "A democracy more perfect than antiquity had dared to dream of started in full size and panoply from the midst of ancient feudal society."

The Plymouth Colony was far from being a perfect democracy, and the Massachusetts Bay Colony made no pretense to being one. Though the Pilgrims experimented for a short while with a kind of primitive communism (taking their communitarian script from the Acts of the Apostles in the New Testament), the basis for a strict hierarchy was present from the beginning. From the covenant theology of Governor William Bradford quickly developed elements suggestive of a rigid theocracy. The form of governance that emerged in Massachusetts was neither egalitarian nor democratic. Nonetheless, at the very outset of our history, the Mayflower Compact established the notion upon which our nation would be founded: governments formed by compact derive their power from the terms set by the governed.

In America, religious covenant and civic compact have a similar character and derive from the same source. Each is freely entered into; and, ultimately, the authority for both is granted by higher authority than that which an earthly king can bestow. In practicing their religion and in creating their government, the Pilgrims of Plymouth Colony acted freely, despite the royal imprimatur of their charter. By so doing they sounded the keynote of American democracy. To cast this point in language that the Pilgrims themselves would have understood, America is founded on the theological conviction that "God's will" and "man's weal" are one and the same.

From hard acquaintance with the tyranny of state-sponsored religion, in establishing their "civil politic" the Pilgrims were motivated by a desire to separate their church from England's state. The Puritans (who came to Boston ten years later and set the tone for New England society) felt no such compunction. Yet they too laid the foundation for the American Creed. Congregational polity—a priesthood of all believers—leads directly to the idea of democratic government. And the practice of religious liberty naturally suggests (and, to a degree, mandates) its correlate, civil liberty. If the Puritans failed to make these connections themselves, their primary commitments to congregational polity and their own religious liberty certainly facilitated the speed and manner in which they were later made.

John Winthrop, first governor of the Massachusetts Bay Colony and leader of the party that arrived in Salem Harbor on eleven ships in 1630, delivered a sermon onboard the flagship *Arbella* shortly before its passengers disembarked to found the city of Boston. Winthrop was a Christian layperson, but among his fellow Puritans this status in no way compromised his spiritual authority. Foreshadowing the development of America's egalitarian spirit, the Puritans (though far from egalitarian themselves) vested moral authority not in an individual's office but in that person's demonstrated virtue. Christian virtue was, in fact, the subtext for Winthrop's sermon. Entitling it "A Model of Christian Charity," he framed the challenge his people faced in purely spiritual terms.

Winthrop knew that he and his company of Puritans were "doing a new thing." He believed that what they were doing was, literally, of cosmic importance. The community they were about to establish would be a beacon for the world, a model for societies everywhere. When one considers the modesty of the enterprise—and that this beacon would be shining three thousand miles away from where anyone could see it—one might justifiably accuse Winthrop of grandiosity. This same charge has been made against America throughout the course of its history. Yet 372 years later, the moral foundation on which Winthrop based his confidence illustrates the nature of our aspirations as a people remarkably well.

If Winthrop's sermon sets the tone for all subsequent expressions of American moral ambition, he could not conceivably have imagined how his Puritan aspirations might one day give rise to a nation dedicated to the celebration of religious pluralism. But faith and freedom ring together in Winthrop's sermon as clearly as they do in the Mayflower Compact. The nation's motto, *E pluribus unum,* echoes throughout, especially in Winthrop's peroration: "We must delight in each other, make others' conditions our own and rejoice together, mourn together, labor and suffer together, always having before our eyes our commission and common work, our community as members of the same body. . . . For we must consider that we shall be like a City upon a Hill; the eyes of all people are on us."

Winthrop's model for society was a biblical one. "The city on a hill that cannot be hid" is Jesus' description of the messianic community from his Sermon on the Mount. But Winthrop also drew his blueprint from the church envisioned by St. Paul, a sacred community of one body with many members. In Paul's Christ there was neither Greek nor Jew, slave nor free, male nor female. So understood, the church had no respect for persons, meaning simply that every person must be treated with equal dignity. Winthrop and his fellow Puritans restricted membership in the one body to those who embraced their own faith's strictures ("the messianic community"), but Paul's metaphor lent itself naturally to more generous subsequent interpretation.

Until his death in 1649, Winthrop governed with moderation. In fact, on account of his leniency he fell from favor and, for a brief time, from major office. Nonetheless, Winthrop's political philosophy was elitist to the core, presuming the superior judgment of a chosen few, in whose hands the fortunes of the community would safely rest. He spoke often of religious liberty but not in such a way that it might be misconstrued as "mere democracy," which represented for him the "meanest and worst of all forms of government." For Winthrop—who believed humanity to be by nature sinful—the word *liberty,* as a human rather than a divine attribute, was interchangeable with the word *license.* Untethered to a directing authority, liberty would lead to immoral behavior and, in turn, undermine social stability. The liberty Winthrop endorsed was "the liberty to that only which is good, just, and honest. This liberty you are to stand for, with the hazard not only of your goods, but of your lives, if need be." Without strong civil and ecclesiastical guidance, the cultivation of such liberty was unimaginable to him.

Winthrop's contemporary, the theologian and historian Cotton Mather, called him the American Nehemiah (a great biblical administrator). Because of his Puritan temperament, revisionists have since excoriated Winthrop for being self-righteous and judgmental, even "un-American." This epithet is unfair. By stressing charity in human relations, Winthrop set a high standard. And, by linking liberty with morality, he offered a chastening reminder that freedom alone is a mixed blessing. Uninformed by morality, freedom is, at best, a neutral value and not a virtue. If there is little "American" about the so-called theocracy Winthrop envisioned and attempted to establish, neither is there anything distinctly "American" about liberty uncoupled with moral suasion.

Before the seventeenth century was half over, Roger Williams and others had already invested the Puritan letter with a broader Christian spirit. In fostering complete religious freedom in Rhode Island, Williams signaled the beginning of the end for established churches throughout the colonies. And, by the close of the seventeenth century, with the introduction of the Quaker faith, William Penn and others had brought a Christianity infused with the spirit of democracy to Pennsylvania. But it was the Pilgrims (despite their modest numbers) and the Puritans (notwithstanding the exclusive nature of their theological vision) who contributed the first important chapter in the development of the American Creed. The principles stated in the Declaration of Independence are a natural extension of covenant theology from congregation to nation as much as they are an inspired adaptation of Enlightenment thought.

With redemptive and ironic consequence, the dance of American faith and freedom couples liberal and evangelistic choreography throughout the course of the nation's history. In 1833, Massachusetts was the last state in the union to disestablish religion, making Unitarianism—today steadfast in its devotion to church/state separation—the American faith last to hold government sanction. The First Church in Plymouth (now Unitarian Universalist) has gathered for 382 years under the Puritan covenant of the Mayflower Compact. Other liberal churches have adapted the Mayflower Compact as their bond of union. In one free translation, the theological letter has been changed so completely as to be almost unrecognizable, yet the source is clear and the spirit still rings true.

We pledge to walk together
In the ways of truth and affection,
As best we know them now
Or may learn them in days to come,
That we and our children may be fulfilled
And that we may speak to the world
In words and actions
Of peace and goodwill.

What Americans of every faith celebrate today at Thanksgiving is more encompassing than what the Pilgrims and Puritans brought with them to the table. But without what they brought, there would be no feast.

2

Soul Freedom

All men may walk as their consciences persuade them,
every one in the name of his God.

—*Rhode Island Code of Laws, 1647*

ALTHOUGH THE PURITAN LEADERS OF MASSACHUSETTS WERE UN-
sympathetic to such later American principles as religious freedom and freedom of speech, the institutions they established and
ideals on which they built these institutions would facilitate the
development of liberal democracy and First Amendment rights.
To call early-seventeenth-century New England a theocracy—if
by this one means the rule of priests—is misleading. Governance
rested in the hands of elected congregants, not those of their
ministerial leaders. The Mayflower Compact was drawn up
wholly without benefit of clergy, the Pilgrims' pastor, John Rob-
inson, having stayed behind in Leiden to tend the majority of
his flock. Four years later, when the home church finally did
dispatch a minister to the colonies, the congregation found him
morally and theologically unsuitable and exiled him in disgrace.
Not until 1629 was a minister settled in Plymouth.

Even then, holy worship continued to be loose in structure.
Despite often severe consequences should one overstep the line
of decency—pillory being among the milder punishments or-

dained for blasphemous behavior or impious speech—worship was remarkably democratic. Psalms were chanted in the most chaotic form imaginable, each congregant taking one line and belting it out freestyle. Worship at times resembled a town meeting, with participants invited to express their interpretations of the day's scripture. This innovative format is evident from an entry in Governor Winthrop's diary. In 1631, on a visit to Plymouth in the company of his minister, John Wilson, Winthrop described a service much freer in form than most Protestant services are today.

> On the Lord's day there was a sacrament, which they did partake in; and in the afternoon, Mr. Roger Williams propounded a question to which the pastor, Mr. Smith, spoke briefly; then Mr. Williams prophesied; and then the governor of Plymouth spoke to the question; after him the elder, Brewster; then some two or three more of the congregation. Then the elder desired the governor of Massachusetts and Mr. Wilson to speak to it, which they did. When this was ended, the deacon, Mr. Fuller, put the congregation in mind of their duty of contribution; whereupon the governor and all the rest went down to the deacon's seat, and put into the box, and then returned.

I wonder what Roger Williams prophesied. No doubt it raised hackles. If congregational polity anticipates American democracy in one respect, Williams's devotion to "soul freedom" shaped our tradition as dramatically. Like Winthrop's Puritans, Williams too was doing a new thing in America. In the suggestively named Providence Plantation, he inaugurated the spirit of American pluralism by enforcing religious toleration.

As reverent to the spirit of the scriptures as Winthrop was to their letter, Williams was committed to religious toleration without in any way being religiously indifferent. To him, free association and expression were essential conditions for genuine religious conviction. For truth to be embraced, it could not be coerced. In Williams's view, governments are established not for the enforcement of religion, but "for the preservation of mankind in civil order and peace. The world otherwise would be like the sea, wherein men, like fishes, would hunt and devour each other, and the greater devour the less."

Roger Williams's career is emblematic of America's emerging democratic spirit. Born in London in 1603 and educated at Cambridge, he arrived in Massachusetts in 1631, six months after Winthrop's flotilla. He was only twenty-seven years old, but his reputation as a minister preceded him, and all expectations were that he would take up his ministry at First Church in Boston, where Winthrop worshiped. Called to this position, he declined. A firm Separatist, he refused to serve any congregation that had not fully and emphatically severed itself from the established church. While rejecting the pomp and ceremony of the Church of England and assembling according to congregational principles, the Puritans were not Separatists. They continued to consider the Church of England their "dear mother," a relationship Williams found intolerable.

He also had no use for Sabbath laws and was the first American to oppose them. In November 1630, shortly before Williams arrived in Boston, a local resident by the name of John Baker was whipped for hunting on the Sabbath. Baker thus became not only the first person to be punished under the Sabbath law of the Massachusetts Bay Colony but, of greater importance, a lightning rod for Williams's campaign to strike all Sunday laws from the books. In mid-1631, Governor Winthrop wrote in his journal that "Mr. Williams had declared his opinion that the magistrate might not punish the breach of the Sabbath, nor any other offense [that was religious], as it was a breach of the first table [of the Ten Commandments]." This was the kind of "novelty" that forced Williams out of Boston.

Just as he burned the last of his Boston bridges, the First Church in Salem called him to serve as their teacher. Thwarted when the Boston authorities lodged a successful protest, Wil-

liams and his wife decided to move to Plymouth. There he as-
sisted the local minister, practiced farming, and traded with the
Indians. This arrangement would prove short-lived. Though in
matters of state Williams was more a Pilgrim than a Puritan,
even the Pilgrims failed to pass his rigorous test of church-state
separation. He certainly failed to pass their test, for they directly
linked civil and religious accountability. William Bradford measured Williams's character in these words: "a man godly and
zealous, having many precious parts, but very unsettled in judgment."

Stemming from a faithful band of Dissenters in England, the
Pilgrims had themselves experienced persecution by the government. Yet, upon arriving in America, Bradford and his fellow
Pilgrims anticipated the Puritans in ensuring that the magiste-
rium of Plymouth Colony would remain in orthodox religious
hands. This arrangement led to a collusion of church and state
similar to the one they had suffered when in the minority—an
irony Williams could not help but point out. Frustrated in Plymouth as he had been in Boston, in 1633 he withdrew from
communion with every church in New England.

Though his stay in Massachusetts was brief, Williams had
created a furor, and not only because of his attitude toward
Sabbath laws and his arch separatist views. He also ran into
trouble with the establishment on account of his outspoken ad-
vocacy of Indian rights. Under the charter of the royal patent,
the Massachusetts Bay Colony could seize Native American lands
without remuneration, a policy Williams vigorously opposed.
In addition, he decried the civil employment of oaths in court
proceedings ("so help me God") and questioned the state's right
both to enforce religious uniformity and to collect taxes to support the clergy. Placed on trial in 1635, he seized the occasion
to accuse his accusers:

> I do affirm it to be against the testimony of Christ
> Jesus for the civil state to impose upon the soul of the
> people a religion, a worship, a ministry. The state
> should give free and absolute permission of conscience

to all men in what is spiritual alone. Ye have lost
yourselves! Your breath blows out the candle of liberty in this land.

Found guilty on both civil and religious grounds, Williams was
banished from Massachusetts.

This punishment was imposed in January, at the very heart
of winter. It could have proved a death sentence. Alone in the
wilderness, Williams might have perished had it not been for
the Native Americans near Narragansett Bay with whom he
found refuge. That summer he purchased (rather than seized) a
parcel of their land and founded the Providence Plantation, there
providing "a shelter to persons distressed for conscience" and
establishing a civil government that would exercise authority
only in civil things.

Other banished Separatists, such as Anne Hutchinson, soon
took refuge with him there. Together they created what Williams fondly referred to as "the lively experiment" of Rhode
Island, otherwise characterized by its religious detractors as
Rogue Island or the sewer of New England. In the words of the
historian George Bancroft, Williams was "the first person in
modern Christendom to establish a civil government on the doctrine of the liberty of conscience, the equality of opinions before
the law. . . . Williams would permit persecution of no opinion,
no religion, leaving heresy unharmed by law, and orthodoxy
unprotected by the terrors of penal statutes."

Hitherto these statutes had been severe. Harsh punishments
continued to be threatened and occasionally imposed throughout
many of the other colonies long after Williams had established
a haven for liberty in Rhode Island. This remains the central
paradox of our early history. Having fled to America in search
of religious liberty, our forebears denied this same liberty to
others, sometimes on pain of death.

Williams rested his defense of religious liberty on three principles: (1) All forms of religious persecution are irreligious; (2)

enforced religious conformity strips belief of conviction and endangers the commonweal; and (3) both institutionally and morally, church and state are protected and thrive only when fully independent from each other. These three points constitute the framework for future separation of church and state in America.

In the first instance, Williams's graphic term for religious persecution was "soul rape." When people are forced to propound what they do not believe, the conscience is ravished and Jesus' message violated. Second, since salvation cannot be coerced, each individual must be permitted the full latitude of his or her conscience in all private matters, especially with respect to religion. Williams offered two reasons for this mandate, one positive and one negative. Religion cannot be authentic without liberty, and those who enforce their own beliefs may be wrong. When wrong, those prosecuting the truth become persecutors of the truth. Williams's insistence on liberty of conscience—with its corollary, tolerance toward those with unpopular opinions— is the keystone for all subsequent legislation protecting minority rights in America, whether religious, social, or political. Williams held that the civil authorities must "provide in their high wisdom for the security of all the respective meetings, assemblings, worshippings, preaching, disputings, etc. . . . [so] that civil peace and the beauty of civility and humanity [may] be maintained among the chief opposers and dissenters."

This proposition undergirds Williams's third argument in favor of religious liberty: It is in the best interest of both church and state for the two to remain independent. To begin with, he could find no warrant in scripture for any such collusion. Did Jesus himself give any indication that, if offered a temporal crown, he would have exercised civil authority or allowed such an authority oversight in spiritual matters? Williams thought not, concluding it must therefore "lamentably be against the testimony of Christ Jesus for the civil state to impose upon the souls of the people a religion, a worship, a ministry, oaths (in religious and civil affairs), tithes, times, days, marryings, and buryings in holy ground."

Freed to make his own distinctions between religious and secular authority, Williams—as John Winthrop noted in his first

complaint—distinguished between the two tables of the Deca-
logue (the Ten Commandments given by God to Moses on Mount
Sinai). The first table concerns our relationship with God. Such
matters fall outside secular jurisdiction. This category affects any
statute regarding blasphemy, heresy, or Sunday observance. The
laws for the second table concern our relationship with our
neighbors. Williams considered these not only religious laws but
also "the law of nature, the law moral and civil," applicable to
all regardless of faith, and constituting the basis for public morality. Accordingly, such laws must be enforced not by religious
but by secular magistrates. The magistrates need not be Christian
in order to adjudicate these laws rightly, for being Christian
bestows no special advantage when it comes to questions of natural law. As Williams himself put it:

> There is a moral virtue, a moral fidelity, ability, and
> honesty, which other men (beside church-members)
> are, by good nature and education, by good laws and
> good examples nourished and trained up in, that civil
> places need not be monopolized into the hands of
> church-members (who sometimes are not fitted for
> them), and all others deprived of their natural and
> civil rights and liberties.

By this light, religious belief is incidental to the administration
of civil jurisprudence. To interpret and enforce public laws, a
just-minded pagan possesses greater moral authority than a cor-
rupt Christian. With Williams's innovation—inspired by the
scriptures—a fundamental shift occurs. No longer is the colony
(and later the nation) a Christian colony, for the government is
no longer a Christian government.

It was thus on religious, not secular, grounds that Roger Williams established the basis for American pluralism. He expressed
his position succinctly in an exchange with John Cotton, then
minister of First Church in Boston and a spirited defender of
established religion in Massachusetts. Cotton claimed that "no

good Christian, much less a good magistrate, can be ignorant of the Principles of saving truth." Williams replied: "This assertion, confounding the nature of civil and moral goodness with religious, is as far from goodness, as darkness is from light."

Williams's legacy is etched in the early records of Rhode Island. The Providence Compact of 1636 explicitly states that all laws to be enacted for the public good would obtain with respect to only "civil things," not religious. In 1640 the Providence Plantation agreement confirmed this pledge: "As formerly hath been the liberties of the town, so still, to hold forth liberty of conscience." In 1643, Williams traveled to England to secure a charter for Rhode Island and win assurances of protection against any interference in its affairs by the Puritans of Massachusetts. Four years later the Rhode Island General Assembly drew up a code of laws culminating in the famous religious liberty clause, granting freedom of conscience in all matters of religious faith and practice.

The laws Williams established in Rhode Island exhibited a more tolerant spirit than he himself did. He was virulently anti-Catholic and recoiled at the Quakers' sometimes uninhibited religious practices (especially the public nudity practiced on rare occasions by completely liberated souls) citing them as proof that Quakers were possessed by the Devil. Yet because of his own laws, Williams's scruples received no public mandate. By the 1670s, Quakers outnumbered Baptists in Rhode Island and had taken over the Provincial Assembly.

In 1774, just before the American Revolution, a new meetinghouse was erected for Williams's old church in Providence. The following year they dedicated their bell, having first engraved on it the following inscription:

For freedom of conscience, the town was first planted,
Persuasion, not force, was used by the people.
This church is the eldest, and has not recanted,
Enjoying and granting, bell, temple, and steeple.

With this telling yet harmonious variation on the Liberty Bell motto ("Proclaim liberty throughout all the land unto all the inhabitants thereof"), Williams's bell pealed forth to all the promise of religious and civil liberty. In the forge of his spiritual imagination, the American Creed had begun to take shape.

3

THE LIBERTY BELL

Let the pulpit resound with the doctrines and sentiments of religious liberty. . . . Let us see delineated
before us the true map of man. Let us hear the dignity
of his nature, and the noble rank he holds among the
works of God—and that God Almighty has promulgated from heaven, liberty, peace, and goodwill to
man!

—John Adams,
"Essay on Feudal and Canon Law," 1765

COMMISSIONED FOR THE PENNSYLVANIA STATEHOUSE IN 1751 TO
mark the Golden Jubilee of William Penn's Charter of Privi-
leges, the Liberty Bell symbolizes American freedom. It did not,
as legend has it, toll to commemorate the adoption of the Declaration of Independence. By prearranged signal (a herald posted
on the steps who shouted, "Ring! Ring!), the bell that witnessed
freedom in Philadelphia on July 4 was in the belfry of nearby
Christ Church. But it did stand sentinel as the Second Continental Congress performed its momentous work. And it pealed
forth clearly eleven years later, when, on September 17, 1787,
Congress met in Philadelphia to adopt the federal Constitution.

Before it rang true, the Liberty Bell had to be cast three times—once to no one's satisfaction by a foundry in England, and twice more in America—until they finally set it right. The Liberty Bell is like our history.

When they chose the wording to be engraved in a band encircling the bell's circumference, the Pennsylvania legislators—at the recommendation of a Quaker delegate—selected these words from Leviticus: "Proclaim liberty throughout all the land unto all the inhabitants thereof." By so doing, they pledged themselves to as expansive a mission as any people could possibly undertake: the establishment of a society based on liberty for all.

The Pennsylvania legislators were mindful of the biblical context from which this proclamation is taken. The twenty-fifth chapter of Leviticus contains Yahweh's declaration to Moses on Mount Sinai of the coming "acceptable year of the Lord." By God's own promise, this intended Jubilee is not a year of wrath but a golden age of reconciliation. In Leviticus, God proclaims that the coming Kingdom will be a time of peace and plenty, with all Heaven's children given equal cause to celebrate. On the promised day of rest, slaves will be freed, old debts forgiven, and society established on a divine footing. Especially appropriate to the fiftieth anniversary of a colony that welcomed people who had been persecuted and jailed in their homelands, the scripture reads: "Ye shall hallow the fiftieth year, and proclaim liberty throughout all the lands unto all the inhabitants thereof: and ye shall return every man unto his possession, and ye shall return every man unto his family."

The Pennsylvania Quakers' view of God's reign pointed to an age not of judgment but of mercy, with liberty bestowed on everyone. At the Jubilee, a new Eden would spring forth, and peace would at last be established on the earth. This long-awaited land of milk and honey would manifest itself in the New World of America, indeed in the colony of Pennsylvania. Twentieth-century fundamentalists may feast their imaginations on the apocalypse, awaiting the earth's destruction and their own transport to Heaven in a state of rapture. Seventeenth-century American Quakers looked toward the Jubilee.

*   *   *

Many of our country's first immigrants fashioned America to be the Promised Land. To assist in its making, they sought divine guidance. As often is the case when scripture is consulted, interpretations concerning what might be construed as divinely sanctioned governance differed markedly from colony to colony. The Puritans labored to establish God's Kingdom on earth; Quakers envisioned this same Kingdom as a commonwealth. The Puritans replaced ecclesiastical authority with the authority of the Bible, but the Quakers went one step further, looking to the oracle within each human soul, which they called an inner light.

In the second half of the seventeenth century, following the lead of their founder, George Fox, the Society of Friends (first in England and then in America) was the most radical and reviled sect in Christendom. Rejecting both church and clergy, they truly democratized the religious spirit. Unlike the Puritans, they also celebrated ethnic pluralism. From modest beginnings in the Delaware Valley and West Jersey, powered by a surge of immigrants from England, Ireland, Wales, Holland, and Germany, at their peak (in the mid-eighteenth century), Quakers had become the third largest denomination in the colonies. Over the next seventy-five years their influence waned. In a search for ever greater moral perfection, they gradually sequestered themselves from the larger society. Yet, from the very beginning, the Quakers' goal was not dominion but peaceable coexistence. Adding their self-described "holy experiment" to Williams's "lively experiment," under the leadership of William Penn they advanced what a century later would most closely approximate the American experiment. Pennsylvania became the laboratory for America.

Penn was as devoted to liberty as Williams and more expansive in his neighborly affections. A friend of John Locke, he didn't embrace Enlightenment thinking as unconditionally as Benjamin Franklin would a century later, but he did establish in Pennsylvania the most humane civil code ever to be incorporated by a government. Penn's first draft for Pennsylvania was the tiny province of West Jersey, whose charter he drew up in

1672 at the age of twenty-eight. Anticipating Locke and employing words suggestive of Jefferson's language in the Declaration of Independence, Penn argued that no one can "take away the Liberty and Property of any (which are natural rights) without breaking the law of nature." Having been arrested for preaching in the streets, he was particularly concerned about the relationship between civil and religious liberty. He published a popular, pamphlet-size book (*English Liberties; or, The Freeborn Subject's Inheritance*) expressly to defend American freedom, both civil and religious. To Penn, English liberties were universal rights established by natural law, which every man and woman is "heir unto by birthright."

Born into circumstances suited for pluralism, William Penn sprang from the English gentry, was raised in Ireland, and thought himself to be of Welsh descent. Having been reared in a military household (his father was an admiral), he initially prepared for a career in the military and distinguished himself in warfare as a youth. Pious by nature and militant in disposition, Penn was expelled from Oxford for his nonconformist views. He wrote several Quaker tracts, witnessed to his faith throughout England, and was imprisoned repeatedly in the Tower of London for his beliefs. Penn's faith led him next to Germany to join arms with persecuted German Pietists and then to America. Having accumulated what for many would be a lifetime of experience, he arrived on the coast of Delaware at the age of twenty-two.

William Penn's story is rich in paradox. Trained to be a soldier, he embraced pacifism. Enrolled at Christ Church College at Oxford (an Anglican bastion), he left a nonconformist and became a committed Quaker. An apostle of simple living, he married an heiress. Unimpressed by the authority of science, he was elected to the British Royal Society. Devoted to liberty, he maintained close relations with two English monarchs (Charles II and James II). When Penn petitioned for a larger province to accommodate the growing number of persecuted Christians from Europe who sought refuge in America, in 1681 Charles II granted him a royal charter (over the objections of his advisers), himself adding "Penn" to the original charter's designation, "Sylvania."

The Quaker experiment was pacific in temperament, democratic in spirit, and neighborly in affection. Whereas Puritans were guided by an abiding conviction of human sinfulness, Friends espoused as deep a faith in natural goodness. Permitted to shine (undirected by theological authorities), the inner light would lead those who followed it to the creation of an ever more compassionate commonwealth. Pennsylvania prospered in large measure thanks to the freedoms that drew a diverse group of religious immigrants to seek peace and liberty there.

Ralph Waldo Emerson said that every institution is "the lengthened shadow of one man." Pennsylvania stands in two men's lengthened shadows. If William Penn coined Pennsylvania, Benjamin Franklin invested it with Enlightenment values, influencing its character and institutions (from schools to scientific societies) with almost limitless practical enthusiasm. Boston-born in 1706 into the household of a soap and candle maker, he was initially designated by his father for the clergy where, as the tenth son (of seventeen children), he would serve as the family tithe. Economic exigencies rendered this pious intention impractical, and young Ben instead apprenticed with his brother as a printer. Introduced to the world of books, he burned his father's candles late into the night, commencing a lifelong pursuit of knowledge. As disciplined as he was curious, Franklin grew up to become our country's most renowned and distinguished citizen, the very embodiment of New World panache. He was our first and greatest self-help guru, the country's preeminent scientist, and its premier diplomat. The most worldly of our nation's founders, Franklin was in no sense a spiritual man. Yet he is as responsible for shaping the American Creed as were John Winthrop, Roger Williams, and William Penn.

The first of our founders to speak in terms of a common faith, Franklin was a pragmatic universalist as much as he was a theological Deist. The union of faith and freedom he envisioned was religious in nature but pluralistic in practice, its shared ethic more important than any single theological expression. Franklin first articulated his vision of a "public religion" in his 1749 "Proposals Relating to the Education of Youth in Pennsylvania," where he advocated the social utility of a morally grounded but nondoctrinal public piety. His most successful contribution to this effort, *Poor Richard's Almanack,* was quintessential American scripture, practical and moral rather than philosophical or theological in content. An annotated commonplace book, Franklin's almanac was full of edifying tidbits and charming, if always didactic, anecdotes. Though he didn't romanticize human nature, with Penn, Franklin believed in human goodness. Properly tutored, common people could—through self-improvement and education—create together an uncommon society.

A true American dreamer, Franklin was as incorrigible an optimist as the world had yet encountered. Nonetheless, even he could not see clearly into the American future. In 1760 he lamented that the colonies "are not only under different governors, but have different forms of government, different laws, different interests, and some of them different religious persuasions and different manners." In Franklin's eyes, a surplus of *pluribus* made *unum* an impossibility. "Their jealousy of each other is so great that, however necessary a union of the colonies has long been for their common defense and security, there are so many causes that must operate to prevent it that, I will venture to say, a union amongst them for such a purpose is not merely improbable, it is impossible."

Knowing how the American story turned out, we can easily overlook how unlikely a story it is. *E pluribus unum* cut directly against the grain of all previous human experience. "One over many" was familiar to history, as were "over many a few" and "some apart from others," but "out of many, one" had no historical precedent. When it came to human liberty, Franklin could not help but wonder how one bell could ring for all. Nonetheless, by the time he took his seat in the Continental Congress, there was no more radical voice for independence than that of Benjamin Franklin. Despite his advanced age, he "did not hesitate at our boldest measures," marveled John Adams, "but rather seems to think us too irresolute and backward."

If American faith was democratized by freedom, freedom finally was secured in considerable measure by the urgings of evangelical faith. William Penn and Benjamin Franklin together created in Pennsylvania a blueprint for eventual American union. By themselves, however, the philosophical ruminations of Quaker idealists and Enlightenment thinkers could never have ignited the revolutionary firestorm that swept the country throughout the 1770s. Secular historians tend to neglect the role orthodox Christianity played in fostering a spirit conducive to revolution. That spirit was kindled as much, if not more, by the religious legacy of the Great Awakening as by the temper of liberal thought.

The evangelical prophets who fired American passions in the mid-eighteenth century were anything but liberal state builders. Yet they too were true apostles of liberty. Revival preaching and hymn singing (more effective agents of rebellion than reason ever could be) set spirits throughout America soaring in ecstasy. Far more persuasively than could a belief in human goodness, the evangelical crusade against evil—enlisting Christian soldiers across the land—prepared recruits for the struggle to follow. If apostles of religious tolerance and civil liberty fashioned the model for the American Creed, it was the radical intolerance of New Light evangelists, fulminating against the evils of the age, that shook the old foundations. Reading the signs of the times with apocalyptic fervor, the evangelical preacher Jonathan Mayhew proclaimed that "great revolutions were at hand." Such passion was catalytic. John Adams himself credited the revolution to a change in Americans' sentiments of their religious obligations and duties. Evangelical zeal fostered the fervor to bring down the walls of tyranny.

The Great Awakening advanced the prospects for the emergence of the American Creed in a second way as well. By now nearly as devoted to religious liberty as were their liberal contemporaries, the apostles of revival envisioned a society transfigured by confessing believers into a "new union." The architect for this vision was Jonathan Edwards. Powerful of mind, animate in spirit, and gifted with eloquence unprecedented in American experience, Edwards was not only our nation's greatest theologian, but also its first literary genius. The imperatives of his teaching led to the founding of Princeton and Rutgers Colleges. And in churches throughout the land his gospel inspired Presbyterians, Baptists, Congregationalists, and Methodists alike to new heights of devotion.

Edwards was born in 1703 in East Windsor, Connecticut. Reflecting the pattern of the times, his education received special attention denied to his nine sisters, and at twelve years of age he entered Yale. A college graduate at sixteen and certified preacher before he turned twenty, Edwards quickly established himself as the preeminent young clergyman of his generation. Almost uniquely, and with persuasive power, he invested orthodox Calvinist faith with Enlightenment insights, drawing directly upon John Locke's rationalism to support the logic of his Christian piety. This combination of influences—enhanced by his innate appreciation for God's indwelling presence through all creation—led him to sound nature's sacred depths. Edwards viewed the natural world not as an enemy to be subdued (as most Puritans had) but as a world charged with enchantment testifying to God's handiwork. Nature's God was as palpable to Edwards as was the God revealed by scripture.

Edwards held fast to a belief in human sin, with the promise of redemption offered only to those who surrender to Christ. Powered by this conviction, by the mid-1730s he kindled a revival in his North Hampton parish that quickly spread across New England. By his own observation, manifestations of the spirit in religious conversion had an uplifting effect on society at large, leading to an increase in charity and moral reform. When his spiritual standards grew too lofty for leaders in his parish, Edwards moved to Stockbridge, Massachusetts, devoting much of his ministry to Native Americans. Named president of Princeton College in 1757, he died shortly thereafter, having left an indelible imprint on the American character.

To Edwards, American faith was integral to American free-dom. "A civil union, or an harmonious agreement among men in the management of their secular concerns is amiable," he ob-served, "but much more a pious union, and sweet agreement in the great business for which man was created, even the business of religion; the life and soul of which is love." Binding together Jesus' great commandments of love to God and love to neighbor, Edwards enhanced his neighbors' understanding of their cove-nant with one another.

Following in the Puritan tradition, he also preached the im-portance of self-criticism—a rigorous and constant moral inven-tory—to ensure that self-interest not obscure the common good. This too is an essential component of the American Creed. Hold-ing each person responsible, at least in part, for the welfare of all, Edwards elevated liberty by linking it with moral account-ability. Once this ethic was given religious voice, more than a building block was added to the concept of *E pluribus unum*. What our union received from the first Great Awakening was its second cornerstone.

Cosponsored by the Methodist evangelist George Whitefield (who drew unprecedented crowds of 10,000 people or more in Philadelphia and Boston in 1739–40), the revival that followed in answer to Edwards's call was the first mass movement in American history. To determine the size of one crowd, Franklin calculated the number of people who possibly could fit within earshot of the Court House steps in Philadelphia, speculating that on one occasion as many as 25,000 people might have gath-ered to hear Whitefield. Franklin was Whitefield's printer and the two became good friends.

Though not swept up in the popular enthusiasm himself, Franklin was witnessing a revival that would enlist thousands of new Americans to freedom's cause. Born-again in Jesus, many were also reborn to a distrust of received authority, infusing pre-Revolutionary America with a radical social, spiritual, and po-litical dynamic. Their suspicions further weakened the grip British monarchy held on American hearts. The British under-secretary of state William Knox complained, "Every man being thus allowed to be his own Pope, he becomes disposed to wish to become his own King." When the crown attempted to reestablish religious order by exporting leading Anglican clergy to help enforce the hegemony of British colonial governors, it only stirred an already roiling pot. Even a majority of Anglicans in Virginia rebelled at this ploy. In all, the spread and vitality of religious pluralism in eighteenth-century America was as instrumental to the founders' proclamation of religious liberty as were the laws of Pennsylvania and Rhode Island that established the legal principle of toleration.

Nonetheless, that Benjamin Franklin and not Jonathan Edwards should face the coin whose obverse is the Liberty Bell is fully appropriate. Edwards would have had little problem with Jefferson's theological language in the declaration. He too viewed God as the God of nature. But he placed a decidedly more Christian emphasis on the term "nature's God" than did Franklin and Jefferson (or even Roger Williams). Embracing theological differences by emphasizing deeds not creeds, Franklin's "public religion" offers a more enduring model for American pluralism than does Edwards's "revivalism." Passion may be necessary to foment revolution against tyranny, but reason better serves the long-standing purposes of a free society. Though it might never have chanced to be written without the destabilizing stimulus of the Great Awakening, the Declaration of Independence is a product of the Enlightenment. When American preachers, moral philosophers, and politicians began describing the Kingdom of Heaven as a great republic in which all citizens are equal and free, the theology underlying such pronouncements reflected Franklin's liberal values more than it did Edwards's evangelical zeal.

In the evolution of the American Creed, Edwards's and Franklin's moral visions complement each other. Neither believed liberty to be a sufficient foundation for a free society. To Franklin, freedom tempers faith while ennobling it. To Edwards—following in the tradition of his Puritan forebears—faith elevates and justifies freedom. For both men, only a union of faith and freedom could (or would) be worthy to endure.

*   *   *

In 1777, with the British marching on Philadelphia, the Continental Congress recommended, and the Supreme Executive Council agreed and ordered, that all bells be removed and hidden, lest they be stolen by the British and melted down into bullets. A group of patriots took the Liberty Bell to Allentown, Pennsylvania, where it was stored in the basement of the Zion Reformed Church. Once the danger had passed, they returned it to the state house. There it pealed out the surrender of General Cornwallis in Yorktown in 1781. Fifty-four years later, while being rung during the funeral of Chief Justice John Marshall, the Liberty Bell cracked.

That the bell should crack means little. More important to remember is how the Liberty Bell received its name. The symbolically cracked Old Statehouse Bell (as it was known) was rechristened in the late 1830s. Its new, now familiar, name was given by a group of Boston abolitionists. The message they sent to their fellow citizens could not have been clearer. "Proclaim liberty throughout all the land unto *all* the inhabitants thereof."

But we are getting ahead of our story. To be redeemed, liberty first had to be established. Which takes us to July 1776 and the birth of the American Creed.

4

"WE HOLD THESE TRUTHS"

I have sworn on the altar of God, eternal hostility to every form of tyranny over the mind of man.

—*Thomas Jefferson,*
Letter to Benjamin Rush,
September 23, 1800

PEOPLE REMEMBER WHAT JEFFERSON SWORE BUT TEND TO FORGET on whose altar he swore it. Those who don't forget sometimes jump to the conclusion that he had his hand on the Bible when he made this oath. He did not. Jefferson swore eternal hostility to every form of tyranny on the altar of nature's God. Roger Williams and Jonathan Edwards may have buttressed their Christianity by invoking the God of nature, but Jefferson's religious views came straight off the presses of the Enlightenment.

Jefferson was more devout than his detractors imagined. In the book of creation, he saw evidence of a divine hand. Human nature was wrought by the same force, with God placed in every head and heart. At once cosmic architect and collective human conscience, Jefferson's God wrote nature's laws and gave us the means, through reason, to enact them. To Jefferson these laws were self-evident—a late substitution in the Declaration of Independence for "sacred and undeniable." And the rights they confirmed were inalienable (the original "inherent and inalienable" considered a redundancy).

"Do the several lines of propositions contained in one paragraph of the Declaration of Independence serve as a creed?" asks the American religious historian Martin Marty. "Can they be inclusive enough to involve the whole nation and its groups?" With Abraham Lincoln and Martin Luther King, Jr., I believe they do and can. The propositions, or "self-evident" truths, in question are (or should be) familiar to all Americans.

> We hold these truths to be self-evident; that all men are created equal; that they are endowed by their Creator with certain inalienable rights; that among these are life, liberty, and the pursuit of happiness; that to secure these rights, governments are instituted among men, deriving their just powers from the consent of the governed; that whenever any form of government becomes destructive of these ends, it is the right of the people to alter or to abolish it, and to institute new government, laying its foundation on such principles, and organizing its powers in such form as to them shall seem most likely to effect their safety and happiness.

Its primary draftsman, Jefferson later described the Declaration of Independence as "an expression of the American mind," and, on another occasion, as "the genuine effusion of the soul of our country." Jefferson's words stand as a summation of our highest aspirations as a people. What is more, they accomplish this feat with conscious intent. They proclaim *themselves* to be the American Creed.

None of Jefferson's propositions is original, but in 1776, when placed in the context of all previous government charters, these "self-evident" truths were hardly self-evident. In fact, they were unique in the history of statecraft. Never before had government limited or bound itself in such a manner or established itself on so egalitarian a footing. The divine authority for human laws is invoked here in a strikingly novel way. With ambition not unlike the hitherto unprecedented ambition of our first English settlers, Jefferson forged in the Declaration of Independence something altogether new in the annals of statecraft.

A*ll men are created equal and endowed by their Creator with certain inalienable rights.* The Declaration of Independence does not read "Some men are created equal" or "All whites are created equal." And women (slighted in other contemporaneous documents, such as the Constitution) were presupposed in the generic use of *man* and *mankind.* Natural rights belong to all; if they could be abridged in any way, a revolution based upon their exercise would lose much of its moral justification.

For Jefferson, the handmaiden of equality was justice. In his First Inaugural Address, he listed justice first among government's obligations, calling for "equal and exact justice to all men, of whatever state or persuasion, religious or political." The abiding irony of America is how often the claims of equity have been abridged in practice. Original constitutional guarantees covered neither race nor gender, and for this reason, throughout the nation's history, claims of justice haunt the founders' boasts of liberty and equality. No one knew this better than Jefferson himself. Reflecting on slavery (where his personal witness is, at best, hypocritical), he wrote, "Indeed I tremble for my country when I reflect that God is just; that his justice cannot sleep forever."

In the first sentence of the Declaration of Independence, "the separate and equal station" to which free people are entitled is guaranteed by "the laws of nature and of nature's God." Dating back to the Greeks and emerging as the centerpiece of Enlightenment science and philosophy, natural law is read from the script of the creation, which trumps all lesser revelations of God's work and majesty. A year before the American Revolution commenced, Alexander Hamilton wrote, "The sacred rights of mankind are not to be rummaged for among old parchments or musty records. They are written, as with a sunbeam, in the whole volume of human nature, by the hand of Divinity itself, and can never be erased or obscured by mortal power." Looking back on the Declaration of Independence with the entitlement that comes with old age, Jefferson infused Hamilton's poetry with not a little hyperbole: "We had no occasion to search into musty records, to hunt up royal parchments, or to investigate the laws and institutions of a semi-barbarous ancestry. We appealed to those of nature, and found them engraved on our hearts."

Enlightenment philosophers were confident that, under the scrutiny of reason, both natural and moral truth would be made self-evident. "Can we suppose less care to be taken in the Order of the Moral than in the natural System?" Ben Franklin asked with rhetorical flourish. No longer do we share the same confidence. Nonetheless, to the extent the American experiment has proved successful, it has been so because our founders (whether Christian or Deist) believed in a natural order based upon the imperatives of moral law. Many of these gentlemen may have been "infidels" in the narrow sense of the word, but they were not atheists. Though he placed the book of nature above the Bible, even "that notorious atheist" Thomas Paine confessed to a "plain, pure, and unmixed belief of one God."

It is remarkable how congenially Enlightenment and orthodox Christian thought met on the ground established by the American Creed. In 1760 the ecclesiastical historian and Puritan minister Ezra Stiles looked back on his ancestors' errand in the wilderness, describing it as "a grand errand . . . that must never be forgotten." Yet, viewed from Stiles's mid-eighteenth-century vantage point, the bridge of ideas connecting the colonization of America a century and a half before to the invention of America fifteen years later is sturdy and striking.

The right of conscience and private judgement is inalienable; and it is truly the interest of all mankind to unite themselves into one body for the liberty, free exercise, and unmolested enjoyment of this right. . . . Being possessed of the precious jewel of religious liberty, a jewel of inestimable worth, let us prize it highly and esteem it too dear to be parted with on

any terms lest we be again entangled with that yoke
of bondage which our fathers could not, would not,
and God grant that we may never, submit to bear.

In 1784, when Thomas Jefferson visited Yale (where Stiles
was now president), Stiles described him as "a most ingenious
naturalist and philosopher, a truly scientific and learned man,
and every way excellent." This meeting of minds between one
of America's leading clergymen and the freethinking Jefferson
says much about the foundation upon which America's shared
values was built.

Nonetheless, Jefferson and his fellow Deists were more re-
sponsive to science than they were to Christian theology. The
scientific method of trial and error in fact challenged the dog-
matism familiar to religion. "This is the age of experiments,"
Benjamin Franklin wrote. Updating Williams's "lively experiment" and Penn's "holy experiment," Jefferson's "fair experiment" was obedient not to the Bible but to the laws of nature
as he understood them.

Others contested the authority of natural moral law in matters
of governance. Concerned that such sweeping claims would undermine the institution of slavery, John Rutledge of South Carolina dismissed both religious and humanitarian concerns as
having nothing to do with the workings of the state. "Interest
alone is the governing principle with nations," he said. Indeed,
the first law of nature as then widely understood was "self-
preservation." The natural right to protect and defend oneself
took precedence over all other rights. When natural law was
first invoked as a grounds for revolution, it was justified in this
limited sense. Jefferson did not discount the first law of nature,
but (with Locke and others) he expanded the compass of natural
law to establish the nation under a broader moral mandate.

If biased in the direction of science, Jefferson was not ignorant
of contemporary theology. Combining the two, he derived his
understanding of natural law from Newtonian cosmology, the
French philosophes, and the English and Scottish Enlightenment

schools. Jefferson could also have subscribed, if not to the particulars of Immanuel Kant's Idealist philosophy, then certainly to the sentiment Kant expressed when he exclaimed, "Two things fill the mind with ever new and increasing admiration and awe, the oftener and the more steadily we reflect on them: the starry heavens above and the moral law within." Kant championed "that lordly ideal of a universal kingdom of reasonable individuals . . . to which we can only belong if we relate solicitously to one another according to the maxims of freedom as if they were laws of nature." To Jefferson, they *were* laws of nature.

In late-eighteenth-century America, Deism reconfigured Christianity; it did not supplant it. But while Deistic thought adapted the core of Christian ethical values, it also tempered Christianity's theological authority. Positing a benign providence, a universal foundation for morality, and the ideal of civic virtue, Deism viewed the creation as a self-regulating whole, its dispensations available to all, not only to a chosen few. In the words of a popular ballad sung throughout the country in 1776:

> *Great nature's law inspires,*
> *All freeborn souls unite,*
> *While common interest fires*
> *Us to defend our rights.*

These rights include life, liberty, and the pursuit of happiness. The nineteenth-century positivist philosopher Auguste Comte argued that the word rights should be struck from the political lexicon. It is a "theological and metaphysical" conception and should have no place in modern scientific discourse. Even American presidents have not always been immune to Comte's logic. Accepting the Republican nomination for vice president in 1920, Calvin Coolidge said, "Men speak of natural rights, but I challenge anyone to show where in nature any rights existed." That is what laws are for, Coolidge argued. Law creates and protects the rights it establishes.

This concept is un-American, with un-American consequences. When the foundation for law is an arbitrary one, moral
checks and balances are relativized. The rights Jefferson listed in
the Declaration of Independence are certainly open to interpretation, but, according to our founders, their metaphysical basis is
not. The rights with which the Creator endows us are inalienable.
Written laws may abridge them, but such laws lack higher sanction. Only laws that protect rights endowed by nature's God rise
to the highest moral standards.

To Jefferson, life, liberty, and the pursuit of happiness were
interdependent. "The God who gave us life gave us liberty at
the same time," he wrote. "The hand of force may destroy, but
cannot disjoin them." True happiness, in turn, can arise only in
a life free from the shackles of tyranny. In Enlightenment
thought, happiness was a practical virtue; it could be neither
pursued nor practiced apart from the common good. Yet its attainment depended upon liberty. When liberty is abridged, the
resulting order in society may be conducive to security, but the
common good (coupling life to liberty, and liberty to happiness)
is compromised and therefore violated.

Happiness by itself is not a right; in the Declaration of Independence only the "pursuit of happiness" is bequeathed by
God. Here too there are limits. When the happiness of some is
pursued at the expense of others, the common good is violated.
Should one person trample on the rights of another in the pursuit
of his or her own ends, or the majority deny rights to a minority,
government has an obligation to intercede—or stop interceding,
as Jefferson would have it—in order to redress the balance. At
the time, such liberty was more likely to be assured by governmental latitude than by federal mandate. Jefferson was wary of
institutional power, advocating a limited government, for precisely this reason.

When rights collide, where to draw the line between conflicting claims is the never-ending and always imperfectly ad-
judicated responsibility of government. Nonetheless, the
religious foundation for universal human rights as expressed by
reverence for natural law is clearly predicated in the American
Creed. The Puritan minister John Wise (prescient before any of

his coreligionists of the emerging American consensus) said it succinctly in 1707: "The natural equality of men amongst men must be duly favored, in that government was never established by God or nature to give one man a prerogative to insult over another. Therefore in a civil, as well as in a natural, state of being, a just equality is to be indulged, so far as that every man is bound to honor every man, which is agreeable both with nature and religion."

It is to secure these rights that government is instituted among us. Hitherto, the most enlightened system of government existed in Great Britain. In fact—Jefferson's hyperbole of creating America out of wholecloth notwithstanding—many aspects of British common law and parliamentary practice were incorporated into our own Constitution. What the Declaration of Independence did was to elevate government's sights by placing human law on a higher moral pediment. The result was a civil ethic, in which the individual conscience received unprecedented priority. The transcendent point of reference was no longer the sovereign but the people themselves, whose rights are endowed with divine authority. People thus become ends in themselves, not means by which to advance some other person's ends. Far from compromising faith, this emphasis on liberty perfects faith by ceding it full range. The intended result is a reverence for the freedom of others to believe as they will, which can only happen if one's own beliefs are protected.

"Without liberty there can be no virtue," wrote Dr. Benjamin Rush, a signer of the declaration from Pennsylvania known for his republican faith as much as for his scientific acumen. When Jefferson was vice president, he and Rush had lengthy discussions on religion. Out of these emerged the Jefferson Bible, a compilation of Jesus' teachings that Jefferson selected to employ for his evening reflections. Their personal interest in religion extended into the public arena as well. Both men placed religious liberty in the forefront of their philosophy of human rights, and therefore high in their catalog of virtues.

Jefferson's lifelong commitment to religious liberty did not betray a distaste for religion. It was an expression of his religion. He did have little use for religious sectaries. And his felt experience of faith surely was limited. (Enlightenment thought stimulates the mind more than it waters the soul.) But, in Jefferson's case at least, Enlightenment thinking was grounded in a lucid set of deeply held theological propositions. Without them, the American Creed would lack the transcendent referent that invests it with higher authority and also the moral sinew necessary actually to unite a free people.

Assuming that the universal truth of reason would soon triumph over centuries of superstition, Jefferson believed that, by the day of his death, every child born in America would be born Unitarian. Once his fellow citizens considered matters a little more carefully, everyone would surely come to the same religious conclusions he himself had. Fortunately (and I speak as a Unitarian), Jefferson was mistaken. A nation of Unitarians would be a pallid nation indeed. Nonetheless, Jefferson was testifying not to his faith in reason alone but also to the reasonableness of his faith. To Jefferson it made no earthly difference whether another individual believed in "twenty gods or no God [for] it neither picks my pocket, nor breaks my leg." In a world where religion often picks people's pockets and breaks their legs, Jefferson dedicated himself to limiting this danger. Hence his zealous pursuit of legal protections for freedom of belief.

Shortly after becoming governor of Virginia in 1779, Jefferson introduced his Bill for Establishing Religious Freedom. It was one of three things, together with founding the University of Virginia and his authorship of the Declaration of Independence (and not, conspicuously, serving as president of the United States), for which he wished to be remembered. Eight years later, after many deft countermaneuvers by the advocates of established religion, Jefferson's bill was voted into law. It reads, in part: "No man shall be compelled to frequent or support any religious worship, place, or ministry whatsoever, nor shall be enforced, restrained, molested, or burthened in his body or goods, nor shall otherwise suffer, on account of his religious opinions or belief; but . . . men shall be free to profess, and by argument to maintain, their opinions in matters of religion, and . . . the same

shall in no wise diminish, enlarge, or affect their civil capaci-
ties."

In his "Memorial and Remonstrance Against Religious As-
sessments," James Madison (who considered a career in the ministry) cast this same argument in positive religious terms.
Drawing what he called "a line of distinction" between the two,
he argued that—for the sake of church and state both—every
person's religion must be left to his or her own conviction and
conscience. "This right is in its nature an inalienable right,"
Madison wrote. "It is inalienable, because the opinions of men,
depending on the evidence contemplated by their own minds
cannot follow the dictates of other men: It is inalienable also,
because what is here a right towards men, is a duty towards the
Creator."

Looking back on the debates and circumstances leading up to
the codification of the American Creed, what detracts more than
anything from its moral claim on succeeding generations is how
dramatically the founders' stated ideals were betrayed by their
tolerance of slavery. It was not that they were insensitive to the
intrinsic worth of human liberty. Even as the Puritans a century
and a half earlier had championed their own religious freedom
not anybody else's, the same could be said of the founders with
respect to freedom itself. They spoke passionately of liberating
the colonies from abject slavery, yet only a few (John Adams
and Benjamin Franklin among the most prominent) denounced
the bondage liberty's champions themselves imposed. When
Washington declared that he would rather the nation be
drenched in blood than inhabited by slaves, he was speaking of
himself and his fellow plantation owners. Even Franklin spoke
of a crown-appointed governor "blackening" and "negrifying"
the Pennsylvania Assembly by denying calls for American
rights. From England, the literary lion Samuel Johnson posed
the obvious question: "How is it that we hear the loudest yelps
for liberty among the drivers of negroes?"

Jefferson, indicted by his own soaring rhetoric, might better
be described as schizophrenic than hypocritical on the question.

A slaveholder who on his death (unlike Washington) failed to offer manumission to the great majority of his slaves (including the half-sister of his first wife and mother of his children, Sally Hemmings), Jefferson nonetheless gave every indication that he included blacks in the benefice bestowed on all by nature's God. In June of 1776, he proposed then-radical language for the Virginia Declaration that would free from bondage any slave henceforth coming into the country. Reflecting on his failure to win passage for this clause, he wrote, "Nothing is more certainly written in the book of fate than that these people are to be free." Expressing astonishment that individuals who would do anything to liberate themselves from the bondage of taxation without representation apparently thought nothing of inflicting actual slavery upon another human being, Jefferson—without a hint of self-recognition—mused openly about how "incomprehensible" human nature is. In the Declaration of Independence itself, his fieriest words condemned the king for waging "cruel war against human nature itself" by countenancing the slave trade. Blatantly hypocritical, this passage was cut, to Jefferson's abiding regret.

When Jefferson dropped the word *property* from Locke's familiar list of rights ("life, liberty, and property"), one possible reason redounds to his moral credit. The text that Jefferson appears to have embellished in his preamble to the Declaration was George Mason's Declaration of Rights for Virginians, adopted the month before: "All men are by nature equally free and independent, and have certain inherent rights, of which, when they enter into a state of society, they cannot by any compact deprive or divest their posterity." To Mason, these rights were life, liberty, property, the pursuit of happiness and the ability to secure safety. The condition guaranteeing these rights only to those who had entered "a state of society" was an amendment to Mason's original draft written to ensure that the declaration expressly excluded slaves (who were not considered members of society) from its compass. Property themselves, slaves were seen as human goods not as humans entitled to full participation in the common good. This demeaning nuance is missing from the Declaration of Independence. By eliminating reference to property from his preamble, Jefferson removed a condition he knew to have been recently imposed to qualify the claims for equal status among all people, slave or free. Whatever his intentions, by so doing he secured the integrity of the American Creed.

The Declaration of Independence has grown in iconic significance over the years. During the Revolutionary and early Federal periods, it was rarely cited as American scripture. With the crisis of union and the war to end American slavery, matters changed completely. At our national hour of greatest danger, Abraham Lincoln placed the American Creed squarely in the middle of the national altar. But from the moment of its composition, Americans began to recognize its significance. On July 3, 1776, one day before its adoption, no less an observer than John Adams predicted in a letter to his wife, Abigail, that the anniversary of American Independence would be celebrated as a "day of deliverance" with "pomp and parades, with shows, games, sports, guns, bells, bonfires, and illuminations from one end of the continent to the other, from this time forward forevermore." He was right. The Fourth of July became an American "holy day" almost immediately, with the first celebration in Philadelphia on this date in 1777. Congress established it as a national day of celebration in 1779, instructing their chaplains "to prepare sermons suitable to the occasion." "From the promulgation of this declaration, every thing assumed a new form," the historian David Ramsay wrote a decade later. July fourth was "consecrated by the Americans to religious gratitude," he said. "It is considered by them as the birth day of their freedom."

Thomas Jefferson's reputation has slipped in recent years. Growing scrutiny of his hypocrisy as a high-minded slaveholder and the late-rising star of John Adams have combined to tarnish his memory. Both revisionist schools enhance the understanding of our history, and are therefore to be welcomed. But, as we rectify the balance, we must be wary of not overloading the other side of the scale. Jefferson's words in the Declaration of Independence have contributed more to the rectitude of our nation than all other utterances combined. It was to Jefferson's towering importance as well as to his brilliance that President John Kennedy was alluding when he quipped to a roomful of Nobel laureates that no more eminent assembly had gathered in the White House since Thomas Jefferson had dined there alone. In another toast of sorts—one far more serious but no less telling—Abraham Lincoln wrote: "All honor to Jefferson, . . . to the man who . . . had the coolness, forecast, and capacity to introduce into a merely revolutionary document an abstract truth, . . . and so to embalm it there, that today, and in all coming days, it shall be a rebuke and a stumbling-block to the very harbingers of reappearing tyranny and oppression."

5

"A New Birth of Freedom"

Let us re-adopt the Declaration of Independence, and, with it, the practices and policy which harmonize with it. Let north and south—let all Americans—let all lovers of liberty everywhere—join in the great and good work. If we do this, we shall not only have saved the Union, but we shall have so saved it that the succeeding millions of free happy people, the world over, shall rise up and call us blessed to the latest generations.

—*Abraham Lincoln,*
speech on the Kansas-Nebraska Act, Peoria, Illinois, 1854

ON JULY 4, 1826, FIFTY YEARS TO THE DAY THAT THEY JOINED in Philadelphia to ratify the Declaration of Independence, together again John Adams and Thomas Jefferson entered the democracy of death. That Adams and Jefferson both should die during the course of our nation's Jubilee confirmed their mythic stature. Adams took final comfort that "Thomas Jefferson survives," but Jefferson was already gone, having died earlier that morning. Declaring that "the most prominent act" in both men's lives had been "their participation in the Declaration of Independence," Senator Daniel Webster commemorated this moment with characteristic grandiloquence: "On our fiftieth anniversary, the great day of national jubilee, in the very hour of public rejoicing, in the midst of echoing and reechoing voices of thanksgiving, while their own names were on all tongues, they took their flight together to the world of spirits." Jefferson himself—looking back shortly before his death on the act that gave birth to the nation—perceived a "holy purpose" at work. Congress's facsimile publication of the Declaration to commemorate its Jubilee inspired him to muse on the nation's "reverence for that instrument," viewing the congressional action as "a pledge of adhesion to its principles and of a sacred determination to maintain and perpetuate them."

Both men died fully conscious that the American future might be darker than its past. The abiding problem was slavery. "Can America be glorious in freedom with such a number of human beings so degraded, so oppressed, so wronged, and so bleeding in her bosom?" one preacher asked in his Fourth of July sermon. "Sons of Columbia, are you not this day happy in your freedom? And does not Liberty ask an offering worthy of your Jubilee? . . . Offer then your slaves, and it shall be a Jubilee indeed." Slavery not only continued to flourish for almost forty years longer, but the problems it occasioned (both moral and political) seemed intractable. The second half of the first American century would see the union parted by a sea of blood.

In 1776, reflecting back on the Boston Massacre of six years before, John Adams (who defended the British soldiers charged with murdering American protesters) concluded that "the blood of the martyrs, right or wrong, proved to be the seeds of the congregation." In a letter he wrote Abigail one day before casting his vote for the Declaration of Independence, he projected this principle into the future: "It may be the will of Heaven that America shall suffer calamities still more wasting and distresses yet more dreadful. . . . The furnace of affliction produces refinement in states as well as individuals, and the new governments we are assuming . . . will require a purification of our vices and an augmentation of our virtues or they will be no blessings."

Jefferson welcomed such disruptions more than Adams did. He advocated the ideal of revolution every nineteen years—the span of a generation. Writing to Adams's son-in-law, Jefferson romanticized revolution as an act of renewal. "The tree of liberty must be refreshed from time to time with the blood of patriots and tyrants. It is its natural manure." Not nineteen but thirty-four years would pass between the death of Adams and Jefferson and the bloodiest war in our nation's history.

In 1852, as the storm clouds were gathering, one passionate student who read American history by the light of both the Bible and the Declaration of Independence was invited by the people of Rochester, New York, to deliver the Fourth of July oration in Corinthian Hall. Frederick Douglass was more incredulous than flattered by this unprecedented honor. "What, to the American slave, is your 4th of July?" he asked. It is a sham, he answered, a reminder of daily injustice and cruelty, mocking the founders' commitment to American liberty and equality. "What have I, or those I represent, to do with your national independence?" he thundered. "Are the great principles of political freedom and of natural justice, embodied in that Declaration of Independence, extended to us?" Declaring America false to its past, present, and future, Douglass embraced the American Creed while dismissing Independence Day celebrations as hollow reminders of the great divide between American practice and American ideals, a gulf estranging millions of black Americans from their birthright.

Born into slavery in 1818, with his likely father a Maryland plantation owner, Douglass stole the rudiments of an education (teaching a slave to read was a crime) and experienced a religious awakening at the age of thirteen through his surreptitious study of the Bible. Having escaped slavery, he moved north to Massachusetts and became active in the abolition movement. By the age of thirty-four, when he spoke in Rochester, Douglass had become not only the leading African American advocate for emancipation, but eminent among its most eloquent champions. Ten years later, President Lincoln would say to him in the White House (in a voice loud enough for everyone around them to hear), "There is no man in the country whose opinion I value more than yours." The two men shared a fierce devotion to the ideals on which the nation was founded and as passionate an opposition to the abject betrayal of these ideals by the ongoing practice of slavery. Douglass knew the injustice firsthand. Lincoln had developed his convictions over a lifetime, tutored by an empathetic imagination. Both viewed the Civil War as America's final hope for redemption.

When Julia Ward Howe wrote "The Battle Hymn of the Republic," she called Union soldiers to battle with a Christian trumpet. Between midnight and dawn on November 18, 1861, she set crusader's words to the martial hymn tune "John Brown's Body," creating a fighting song for the Union army to march to through the remaining years of the Civil War. With apocalyptic imagery, Howe envisioned a second coming of the Lord, "trampling out the vintage where the grapes of wrath are stored." God's sword, "terrible" and "swift," would loose its "fateful lightning"; God's "righteous sentence" would be read by campfires' "dim and flaring lamps." Even as the Puritans followed the steps of Moses to a new Promised Land, Howe read her generation's chapter of American history in the light of Jesus' crucifixion and resurrection.

> In the beauty of the lilies Christ was born across the sea,
> With a glory in his bosom that transfigures you and me;
> As he died to make men holy, let us die to make men free,
>   While God is marching on.

Though herself a religious liberal, Howe's words capture something far more primal than the measured cadences of rational religion. Her passion was unleashed by a holy cause: the cause of freedom. For Howe, emancipation and union were inseparable. Freedom transfigured her once dispassionate faith into a battle cry.

Lincoln was initially more concerned about union than he was about slavery. Yet, whenever he thought back on the Declaration of Independence, slavery was foremost in his mind. "Our progress in degeneracy appears to me to be pretty rapid," he wrote in 1855. "As a nation, we began by declaring that '*all men are created equal.*' We now practically read it '*all men are created equal, except negroes.*' " Lincoln adopted this refrain as his mantra. Speaking at Independence Hall in Philadelphia shortly before his inauguration, he lifted up "that sentiment in the Declaration of Independence, which gave liberty not alone to the people of this country, but hope to all the world, for all future time. It was that which gave promise that in due time the weights would be lifted from the shoulders of all men." Honoring our creed by ending slavery could alone save our country. "If it can't be saved upon that principle, it will be truly awful," Lincoln said, adding in an aside, "I would rather be assassinated on this spot than to surrender it."

Lincoln saved American liberty by expanding it, thus advancing the founders' noble but unfinished work. At the same time, he placed himself under higher judgment. Following Jefferson's map (if not his path), Lincoln saw his own and the nation's task as one.

The map itself was clear. Jefferson had asked in his *Notes on the State of Virginia,* "Can the liberties of a nation be thought secure when we have removed their only firm basis, a conviction in the minds of the people that these liberties are of the gift of God?" His conclusion was an ominous one. "They are not to be violated but with His wrath." Speaking directly of the institution of slavery, Jefferson then wrote the poignant, self-judging lines to which I alluded earlier: "Indeed I tremble for my country when I reflect that God is just; that his justice cannot sleep forever," adding that "the Almighty has no attribute which can take side with us in such a contest." Jefferson did not act on this conviction. But he swore on God's altar what Lincoln signed in blood. Not only is slavery a moral wrong; it is also a blatant violation of natural law and therefore a sin against God.

Lincoln honored Jefferson for his ideals. He revered the Declaration of Independence as "a standard maxim for free society," something "constantly looked to, constantly labored for, and, even though never perfectly attained, constantly approximated, and thereby constantly spreading and deepening its influence, and augmenting the happiness and value of life to all people of all colors everywhere." Lincoln's commitment to this guiding principle deepened during the course of the war. By the time of his martyrdom, like Julia Ward Howe he had been transfigured by a zeal for justice. For this reason the death of our sixteenth president, shot on Good Friday, proved as richly symbolic as were the deaths of our second and third.

At the November 19, 1863, dedication of the National Soldiers' Cemetery at Gettysburg, with thousands of soldiers from both sides who gave their lives in early July of that year being ceremoniously laid to rest, Lincoln's role was a minor one. The sponsors invited him to make "a few appropriate remarks" following the major address to be delivered by the Rev. Edward Everett of Massachusetts. Everett, a former U.S. senator and president of Harvard, was the most highly regarded orator of his day. In polished, well-modulated cadences he spoke for two full hours to a crowd of 15,000 on Cemetery Ridge. The Baltimore Glee Club followed by singing a solemn dirge. Only then did Lincoln, his voice reedy but piercing, deliver his two-minute address.

At first the speech had a mixed reception. Secretary of State William Seward turned to Everett on the platform and said, "He has made a failure and I am sorry for it; his speech is not equal to him." Everett disagreed. "Ah, Mr. President," he said, "how gladly would I give my hundred pages to be the author of your twenty lines." The next day he wrote, "I should be glad if I could flatter myself that I came as near to the central idea of the occasion in two hours as you did in two minutes," to which Lincoln replied, "I am pleased to know that, in your judgment, the little I did say was not entirely a failure." In fact, the American Creed has rarely found more eloquent expression.

Fourscore and seven years ago our fathers brought forth on this continent, a new nation, conceived in liberty, and dedicated to the proposition that all men are created equal.

Now, we are engaged in a great Civil War, testing whether that nation or any nation so conceived and so dedicated can long endure. We are met on the bat-tlefield of that war, to dedicate a portion of that field as a final resting place to those who here gave their lives that that nation might live. It is altogether fitting and proper that we should do this.

But, in a larger sense, we cannot dedicate—we cannot consecrate—we cannot hallow—this ground. The brave men, living and dead, who struggled here have consecrated it far above our poor power to add or detract. The world will little note nor long remember what we say here, but it can never forget what they did here. It is for us, the living, rather, to be dedicated here to the unfinished work which they who fought here have thus far so nobly advanced. It is rather for us to be here dedicated to the great task remaining before us—that from these honored dead we take in-creased devotion to that cause for which they gave the last full measure of devotion; that we here highly re-solve that these dead shall not have died in vain; that this nation, under God, shall have a new birth of freedom; and that government of the people, by the people, for the people shall not perish from the earth.

Lincoln's language has a biblical feel, but it stems directly from American writ. Through the sacrifices of its citizens and at the time of its greatest trial, our nation, founded on the proposition that all are born equal and invested with certain inalienable rights, could finally attain its moral promise. The poet Robert Lowell considered the Gettysburg Address sacramental. "In his words, Lincoln symbolically died, just as the Union soldiers really died—and as he himself was soon really to die. By his words, he gave the field of battle a symbolic significance that it had lacked. For us and our country, he left Jefferson's ideals of freedom and equality joined to the Christian sacrificial act of death and rebirth." How appropriate that the victory in Gettysburg should have been won on the nation's birthday, Lincoln told a reporter, "since on the Fourth of July for the first time in the history of the world a nation by its representatives, assembled and declared as a self-evident truth that 'all men are created equal.'"

In the years leading up to the Civil War, both parties—abolitionist and slaveholder alike—defended their antithetical positions by marshaling evidence from the Constitution and the scriptures. Even the Declaration of Independence served two masters for a time, with abolitionists interpreting inclusively the propositional clause that all are created equal, and the pro-slavery party responding that the authors' intention clearly excluded people of color.

This divergence lies at the heart of the 1857 Dred Scott Supreme Court decision. Scott was a slave who served his master in Illinois (where slavery had been outlawed in 1787) and Wisconsin (a free state under the provisions of the Missouri Compromise). Scott argued that—having been resident in these states—he was henceforth a free man. The court disagreed. Rendering the court's opinion, Chief Justice Roger Taney acknowledged that the ruling that Negroes could not be considered citizens and Jefferson's pledge to equality in the Declaration of Independence were at odds. The justices resolved this discrepancy by claiming that "the legislation and histories of the times, and the language used in the Declaration of Independence, show that neither the class of persons who had been imported as slaves nor their descendants, whether they had become free or not, were then acknowledged as a part of the people nor intended to be included in the general words used in that memorable instrument."

Taney confessed that Jefferson's words might appear to embrace the whole human family but dismissed this appearance as an illusion. If true, an otherwise stirring and inspirational document would be transformed into one that instead would deserve and should receive "universal rebuke and reprobation." Since many of our founders themselves held slaves, Taney argued that to claim the Declaration of Independence includes people of color among those created equal and vested with certain inalienable rights is to charge its signers with hypocrisy.

The consequences of the Dred Scott decision were staggering. Among other things, freed slaves (now officially not citizens), could no longer own property even in the North. The federal government invoked this interpretation as late as 1860 to confiscate land owned by black freedmen. With the preamble of the Declaration of Independence twisted into a defense of slavery, the nation's soul was in jeopardy. Lincoln lamented that the Dred Scott decision rendered "the perfect freedom of the people to be just no freedom at all."

In the famous Lincoln-Douglas debates of 1858, Stephen A. Douglas, who defeated Lincoln for the U.S. Senate in Illinois, defended the Dred Scott decision. He admonished Lincoln—and all other critics of this ruling—pointing out that the Supreme Court has unquestionable authority to interpret the Constitution. Whether we like them or not, its decisions should be immune from democratic meddling, he claimed. Douglas held a pure states' rights position (much like those taken to defend segregation during the civil rights debates of the 1950s and 1960s): "I care more for the great principle of self-government, than I do for all the Negroes in Christendom," he said. Then he went straight for the emotional jugular at the heart of many people's support of slavery: "I would not blot out the great inalienable rights of the white men for all the Negroes that ever existed. I do not regard the Negro as my equal, and positively deny that he is my brother or any kin to me whatever."

Douglas capped his rhetoric by enlisting God as a witness for his ungodly cause: "I do not believe that the Almighty ever intended the Negro to be the equal of the white man. If he did, he has been a long time demonstrating the fact. For thousands of years the Negro has been a race upon the earth, and during all that time, in all latitudes and climates, wherever he has wandered or been taken, he has been inferior to the race which he has there met. He belongs to an inferior race and must always occupy an inferior position."

Lincoln could have responded by quoting Isaiah 42 ("He will make justice shine on every race"). But, perceiving the intimate relationship between American democracy and the ideals of equality and justice, he chose instead to cite chapter and verse of the American Creed. "According to our ancient faith, the just powers of governments are derived from the consent of the governed," he said. "Allow ALL the governed an equal voice in the government, . . . that, and that only, is self-government." Charging Douglas with "blowing out the moral lights around us," and with "eradicating the light of reason and the love of liberty in this American people," in a voice thinner but morally far more resonant than that of his eloquent opponent, Lincoln reclaimed the Declaration of Independence from its late captivity. "A house divided against itself cannot stand," he concluded, quoting from the Bible. "I believe, this government cannot endure, permanently, half slave and half free."

Lincoln's star too has fallen in recent years, tugged by the gravity of revisionist accusations that he was himself a white supremacist, different from Douglas in degree but not in kind. It is true that Lincoln conceded his opponent's argument that African Americans were not equal to whites with respect to intellect, moral development, or social capacity. This view was held by the vast majority of his audience, and perhaps to a degree by Lincoln himself, though other testimony disputes that. But his critics overlook the context in which he made such statements. In a debate, one scores points by conceding the strongest arguments martialed by one's opponent. This was Lincoln's strategy—to elevate the ground on which the contest was being waged. Notwithstanding evidence of racial inequalities, he argued in one debate, "there is no reason in the world why the Negro is not entitled to all the natural rights enumerated in the Declaration of Independence, the right to life, liberty and the pursuit of happiness." Quoting the Declaration's proposition that "all men are created equal," he sealed his argument by concluding, "This was [the founders'] majestic interpretation of the economy of the Universe. . . . Nothing stamped with the divine image and likeness was sent into the world to be trodden on, and degraded, and imbruted by its fellows." Lincoln was not without prejudice, but neither was he unwilling to adapt his true feelings in order to strengthen the power of his rhetoric.

Lincoln's religious beliefs were far from conventional. Raised by Freewill Baptists in Kentucky—his father, Thomas, held slavery incompatible with the dictates of religion—the young Lincoln found Thomas Paine's Deism more attractive than his parents' Christianity. But as he grew older, suffering through the deaths of brother, sister, and two sons, and contemplating the carnage of war, Lincoln gradually adopted a more Christian outlook. Even then he held no truck with theologians. "The more a man knew of theology," he once said, "the further he got away from the spirit of Christ." When asked why he refused to join a church, Lincoln replied, "Because I find difficulty without mental reservation in giving my assent to their long and complicated creeds," adding, "When any church inscribes on its altar, as a qualification for membership, the Savior's statement of the substance of the law and the Gospel—'Thou shalt love the Lord thy God with all thy heart and with all thy soul and with all thy mind . . . and thy neighbor as thyself'—that church will I join with all my heart and soul."

He also appears to have been influenced by the affinity his law partner, William H. Herndon, had for the teachings of the transcendentalist preacher Theodore Parker, a leading abolitionist. Parker considered the Declaration of Independence "the great political idea of America," one grounded in natural law and conducive to moral progress. Parker equated the Declaration's relationship to the American Constitution with that of Jesus to the Bible. Both gave spirit to the letter, fostering aspirations that, if risen to, would establish "the reign of righteousness, the kingdom of justice, which all noble hearts long for, and labor to produce, the ideal whereunto mankind slowly draws near."

That the idea of progress (held closer to heart by Parker than by Lincoln) has been dashed on the rocks of unfolding history in no way diminishes the authority of the writ to which both men swore allegiance. So long as the founders' principles were not abandoned—as both believed and Lincoln proclaimed—America would answer to the "better angels of [its] nature."

Another Transcendalist, William Henry Channing (nephew of the more famous William Ellery), had summed up the challenge slavery posed to Americans who would be faithful to their ideals. For all injustices for which we as a people are responsible, the Declaration of Independence holds us accountable, he said. It reminds us of the "peculiar opportunities and duties" that accompany American citizenship. Echoing Jefferson, but expressing more emphatic resolve, Channing wrote:

> We deserve the retributions, losses, disgraces which our savage robberies of the Indians, our cruel and wanton oppressions of the Africans, our unjust habits of white serfdom, our grasping national ambition, our eagerness for wealth, our deceitful modes of external and internal trade, our jealous competitions between different professions and callings, our aping of aristocratic distinctions, our profligate expenditures, public and private, have brought, and will continue to bring upon us.

With Lincoln, Channing believed that the nation is entrusted with a divine mission, "consecrated by the devout faithfulness of forefathers," whose "declaration of principles" was "the clearest announcement of universal rights" in all of history. Because Americans have a text, we can use it to measure how we are doing as a people. That is why Lincoln called the Declaration of Independence "spiritually regenerative."

If influenced by Transcendentalist thought, Linclon stood squarely in the Puritan tradition of self-judgment, believing that we are united not by righteousness but by sin. In this spirit, and—as always—including himself under judgment, he asked (in his 1863 Thanksgiving Proclamation) for everyone to repent "with humble penitence for our national perverseness and dis-obedience." For Lincoln the principal benchmark for our sinful-ness was the extent to which we had failed to live up to the moral imperatives implicit in the national scripture.

Nowhere is this more evident than in his Second Inaugural Address, delivered only months before he died. Looking back over fields of heartbreak and devastation—650,000 American dead, some $10 billion of property damage—Lincoln fulfilled the prophet's ancient role: to speak the word of God without hubris. Considering this address perhaps better than anything he had produced, he did acknowledge that it would not be immediately popular. "Men are not flattered by being shown that there has been a difference of purpose between the Almighty and them."

In an eight-minute speech—between George Washington's First Inaugural and that of George W. Bush, the shortest inau-gural address on record—Lincoln began by acknowledging that during the late conflict between North and South both sides read the same Bible and petitioned the same God for assistance against the other. "It may seem strange that any men should dare to ask a just God's assistance in wringing their bread from the sweat of other men's faces," he said, "but let us judge not that we be not judged." In God's good time, justice would ultimately be done and the ungodly institution of slavery abolished. Even then, however, given our sinful nature, the prayers of neither side would be answered fully. Our judgments are themselves under a higher judgment, one we cannot presume perfectly to discern, whereas "the judgments of the Lord are true and righ-teous altogether."

In closing, Lincoln expresses the essence of Jesus' gospel. The key to the scriptures is to practice neighborly love:

With malice toward none, with charity for all, with firmness in the right as God gives us to see the right, let us strive on to finish the work we are in, to bind up the nation's wounds, to care for him who shall have borne the battle and for his widow and his orphan—to do all which may achieve and cherish a just and lasting peace among ourselves and with all nations.

Congress engraved these words—together with those of the Gettysburg Address—on the walls of the Lincoln Memorial in Washington.

Another symbol in the nation's capital invokes Lincoln's memory, if more obliquely. The American sculptor Thomas Crawford was commissioned in 1855 to design a statue to be placed atop the U.S. Capitol. His proposal ("Freedom Triumphant in War and Peace") depicted Liberty—a woman whose cap was fashioned to recall the ancient Greek symbol of a freed slave. In 1863, the very year Lincoln issued his Emancipation Proclamation, this symbol—though muted when the cap was replaced by a helmet—took her rightful place upon the dome.

By being true to its intentions, Abraham Lincoln's Proclamation consecrated the American Creed, securing his place in the developing American mythos. From the moment of his death, Lincoln was elevated to the pantheon of what Benjamin Franklin called our "public faith," a temple that offers moral instruction to all Americans. Lincoln personified this faith, even as he guided it. "We cannot escape history," Lincoln told his countrymen at the height of the war. "The fiery trial through which we pass, will light us down, in honor or dishonor, to the latest generation. . . . In giving freedom to the slave, we assure freedom to the free—honorable alike in what we give, and what we preserve. We shall nobly save, or meanly lose the last, best hope on earth." Refired but not refashioned in the furnaces of war, the American Creed thus received its most eloquent and enduring statement. Lincoln not only saved the Union. He also redeemed our union of faith and freedom.

6

E Pluribus Unum

[*David's uncle asks:*] What true understanding can there
be between a Russian Jew and a Russian Christian?

DAVID: What understanding? Aren't we both Americans?

—*Israel Zangwill,*
The Melting Pot, 1908

Among the officers Ulysses S. Grant brought with him to
the signing ceremony for the Confederate surrender in Appo-
mattox was Ely Parker, a Seneca Indian. "I'm glad to see one
real American here," Robert E. Lee is reported to have said. To
which Parker diplomatically replied, "We are all Americans."

United once more, America was nonetheless more diverse
than ever. Of our many populations, the Native Americans were
the only segment of the nation in decline. Those who were not
acculturated into the dominant society were being herded tribe
by tribe onto reservations. For all the talk of melting pots in
decades to come, Native Americans were driven into the corner
of the country kitchen, far from the family table.

In other respects, under Lincoln's guidance the nation's mission and identity became clearer. We took a significant step toward becoming one people—the moral justification for that goal
now clearly established with reference to the founders' vision.
North and South united. East and West were being coupled by
rail. Yet the end of slavery had little impact on the persistence

of racism; women had begun to demand equal rights; and—
both ethnically and religiously—the population was becoming
increasingly varied, adding dozens of new tension points to the
body politic. Throughout the century, waves of immigrants enriched American diversity while testing the sustainability of
American pluralism. Far from being a melting pot, America was
a patchwork quilt whose disparate sized and colored squares
were joined in every combination imaginable.

When pondering the impact immigration has had on our nation, we often think first of the tide of Catholics and Jews that
flooded America in the late nineteenth and early twentieth centuries, and of the waves of Latin American and Asian immigrants
that followed. Each of these populations enriched the country in
distinctive ways and brought with them unique challenges. But
the pattern for incorporating new citizens was already well established by 1886, when the Statue of Liberty was dedicated in
New York Harbor. Critical to the success of our ever-changing
nation were the unchanging principles upon which America was
founded.

In his Fourth of July Address delivered in Springfield, Illinois, in 1857, Abraham Lincoln underscored how much the
United States had changed over the previous three-quarters of a
century. Speaking of America's first patriots, he observed to the
crowd, "Quite half of you are not even descendants of those
who are referred to at that day." This became a leitmotiv for
Lincoln, and proof of our founders' genius. Celebrating the
Fourth of July a year later, he said:

> We have, besides these men descended by blood from
> our ancestors, among us perhaps half our people who
> are not descendants at all of these men. . . . They can-
> not carry themselves back into that glorious epoch and
> make themselves feel that they are part of us, but
> when they look through that old Declaration of In-
> dependence they find that those old men say that "we
> hold these truths to be self-evident, that all men are
> created equal," and then they feel that that moral sen-

timent taught in that day evidences their relation to those men, that it is the father of all moral principle in them, and that they have a right to claim it as though they were blood of the blood, and flesh of the flesh of the men who wrote that Declaration, and so they are. That is the electric cord in that Declaration that links the hearts of patriotic and liberty-loving men together.

In a real sense the American republic is a world republic. Whether Americans are, as Lincoln observed, an "almost chosen people," excluding those who were brought here as slaves, we are certainly a self-selected people. With the exception of Native Americans, every American traces his or her roots to people who came here "off the boat." The great majority of new citizens arrived seeking freedom and opportunity. Whether inspired by courage, driven by necessity, or both, many extended their journey yet further, setting out into what remained of the American wilderness.

To accommodate each new wave of immigrants, the nineteenth century saw rapid westward expansion. Freedom's urgings demanded what Daniel Boone called elbow room. As one territory would be colonized, free spirits would take off further west. One characteristic of western expansion was its display of what has been called natural freedom. More than either New Englanders or people from the old South, many westerners exhibited a strong mistrust for institutions, manifesting strident independence. Given how rapidly the West was growing, this libertarian impulse further shaped the character of America.

When George Washington was president, 95 percent of the nation's population resided east of the Allegheny Mountains. As Lincoln was speaking, more than half lived west of the Alleghenies, a percentage that grew steadily over the years to follow. Traveling west, every other wagon contained (alongside the family Bible) a set of McGuffey Readers. These children's textbooks (also read by adults learning English) were chock-full of patriotic anecdote and uplifting moral teaching. A staggering 1 20 million sets of McGuffey Readers were published between 1838 and 1920. Supplemented by Parson Weems's American legends (especially his *Life of Washington*), these primers supplied a common narrative for people whose backgrounds in other respects were remarkably diverse. What held America together was the facility with which each generation of new Americans adopted the nation's history.

William Grimshaw's *History of the United States*—read by Abraham Lincoln and untold numbers of other young Americans—was explicit in summing up that history according to the nation's creed. In a closing flourish, Grimshaw exhorted his readers, "Let us not only declare by words, but demonstrate by our actions that 'all men are created equal; that they are endowed by their creator with the same inalienable rights; that among these are life, liberty, and the pursuit of happiness.' " Popular history and Bible stories were the MTV of generation upon generation of young Americans. Their widespread dissemination and the reverence with which they were transmitted and received endowed the nation with a common civic tongue.

Yet, despite this appearance of unity, the polyphonous nature of belief and its expression were unprecedented. By mid-century, reflecting and stimulating the growth of participatory democracy, the most modest community sponsored dozens of religious and voluntary associations. Take Oregon City, for instance, in 1858 a town of 500 citizens. One visitor observed, "There are two public houses—temperance—two liquor saloons, and one grocery. There are a Methodist Church, Congregational Church, Baptist Church, Catholic Church; the Episcopalians hold regular services. There is a Masonic Lodge, an Oddfellows Lodge and a Division of the Sons of Temperance in the city." From the greatest metropolis to the most remote hamlet, throughout the nineteenth century American pluralism (abetted by the democratic urgings of voluntary association) witnessed ever more expressively the ideal of unity with diversity.

Religious passions were not muted but complemented by the spirit of liberty that held these disparate groups together. This was true for people of all faiths. And religion was rising with the nation's tide. In 1800 only 10 percent of Americans were official members of a church, though more people had strong religious convictions than this statistic might suggest. Especially among those of Puritan leanings, church membership was a very serious covenant. But, by any measure, religious participation grew steadily over the succeeding decades. From the end of the Revolution to the beginning of the Civil War, the population of the country increased eightfold (from 4 to 32 million people), while the number of congregations burgeoned by a factor of twenty (from 2,500 to 52,000) and the number of preachers per capita quadrupled. Throughout the first half of the century, Jews remained few in number, but, from 1800 to 1860, the ranks of Roman Catholics more than doubled.

Religious options proliferated as well. The mainline Protestant churches (Baptist, Presbyterian, Methodist, Lutheran, Episcopal) and various smaller sects (Mennonite, German and Dutch Reformed, Moravian, Quaker) had all been imported from Europe. But in the nineteenth century, spicing the mix, America began to give birth to its own religions (Unitarian, Universalist, Mormon, Christian Science), a process that continues to this day.

In Protestant America, between the turn of the nineteenth century and the eve of the Civil War, the nation experienced what some have called the Second Great Awakening. Given the nature of American revivalism, the spread of evangelical faith brought with it a vitalization of the democratic spirit. Highly participatory in nature, revivals—as they do today—sent a charge through the body politic. "Let the human mind loose," John Adams had urged. Liberated by every manner of spiritual prophet and preacher, during these years the independent American soul flourished no less than had the American mind during the early days of our republic.

The cacophony of opinion characteristic of American experience was evident in nineteenth-century revivals. Evangelists fulminated against the decline of American morality from both right and left. Some proposed revising the Constitution to abridge the separation clause. Liberal Christians, notably the tiny band of Unitarians, led the fight for abolition and women's suffrage. Other sectarians, most emphatically the Millerites—who rallied fifty thousand followers to await the end of the world— invested their hopes in Heaven.

The age was rife with passion, which sometimes led to violence. Mormons were persecuted and their founder, Joseph Smith, was killed by a mob. Fear of "the other"—prompted especially by burgeoning Catholic immigration—also led to temporary gains by nativist groups, such as the Know-Nothing Party, which opposed further immigration. Yet foreign visitors to our country were still struck by the widespread coexistence of religious enthusiasm and religious toleration. Gustave de Beaumont, who traveled for a time with Tocqueville, noted that "this extreme tolerance on the one hand towards religion in general— on the other this considerable zeal of each individual for his own religion, is a phenomenon I can't yet explain to myself."

Once again the explanation may lie in the extent to which liberty was itself a party to religious zeal. The eighteenth-century revivals emerged from the academy and had as considerable an impact on education as they did on popular piety. In contrast, the so-called Second Great Awakening was a populist affair, generating most of its enthusiasm among the poor. But its watchword remained freedom. The nation's spiritual vitality was in no way diminished—in fact, it was facilitated—by the guarantees of religious liberty established by the founders.

While dramatically extending American personal and group identity, nineteenth-century revivals were distinctively American in another way as well. They reinvested our nation as a whole with a moral mission and destiny. Well beyond the precincts of evangelical religion, this unleashing of spiritual energy sparked and facilitated every manner of social activism. In 1840, Ralph Waldo Emerson applied his wit to a description of one assembly of activists who gathered in Boston. Among the participants he encountered at the Chardon Street Convention were "madmen, madwomen, men with beards, Dunkards, Muggletonians, Comeouters, Groaners, Agrarians, Seventh-Day Baptists, Quakers, Abolitionists, Calvinists, Unitarians, Philosophers—all came successively to the top, and seized their moment, if not their hour."

One expression of this social ferment to have lasting consequence was the movement for women's rights. By constitutional
mandate, half the American population had been excluded from
full participation in American democracy. More disenfranchised
even than African American freemen, women didn't win the
right to vote until 1920, with ratification of the Nineteenth
Amendment. In a pivotal moment for American feminism, foremothers in the struggle for women's equality gathered in 1848
in Seneca Falls, New York. Demanding economic, legal, edu-
cational, and moral rights equal to those enjoyed by American
males, determined women led by Elizabeth Cady Stanton and,
later, Susan B. Anthony set the agenda for a movement that
eventually would revolutionize American society. The Declaration of Sentiments ratified in Seneca Falls has a familiar ring.

> When, in the course of human events, it becomes nec-
> essary for one portion of the family of man to assume
> among the people of the earth a position different from
> that which they have hitherto occupied, but one to
> which the laws of nature and of nature's God entitle
> them, a decent respect to the opinions of mankind
> requires that they should declare the causes that impel
> them to such a course.
>
> We hold these truths to be self-evident: that all men
> and women are created equal; that they are endowed
> by their Creator with certain inalienable rights.

Many other reformers—from factory workers to farmers—
recast the Declaration to underscore the legitimacy of their
causes. Its choice as a foundation for their claims makes perfect
sense. In fact, to appreciate the full power of the American
Creed, one almost has to read it through the eyes of those whose
inalienable rights are abridged or denied by governmental writ.
In its various incarnations, American Feminism represents a val-
iant, yet unfinished campaign to tune the nation's history to the

key of its ideals. Symbolic of this struggle and its difficulty, though liberty appears often on national coinage in the guise of a woman, when Congress fashioned a dollar coin with Susan B. Anthony on its face, people mistook it for a quarter. It fell first from favor and then from circulation. This irony suggests a tension between word and deed familiar to women throughout the nation's history.

Early American feminism too spoke in many voices, from the liberal religious language of Stanton and Anthony to the evangelical tongues of the Second Great Awakening, where family concerns raised by wives and mothers outweighed a commitment to individual rights. Then and later, without reference to the American Creed it is difficult to imagine how America's varied moral voices fit into the same register. But the liberties proclaimed as our birthright are encompassing by definition. Forgotten voices are encouraged, discordant ones protected, and those that rise to prophecy uplifted by our creed.

Americans have never been "children of the crucible," as Theodore Roosevelt was to claim after seeing Israel Zangwill's popular play *The Melting Pot* in 1908. Roosevelt was referring to the often-quoted passage in which the protagonist looks out over a crowd at Ellis Island and exclaims:

> America is God's Crucible, the great Melting-Pot where all the races of Europe are melting and reforming! Here you stand, good folk, with your fifty languages and histories, and your fifty blood hatreds and rivalries. But you won't be long like that, brothers, for these are the fires of God you've come to— these are the fires of God. A fig for your feuds and vendettas! Germans and Frenchmen, Irishmen and Englishmen, Jews and Russians—into the Crucible with you all! God is making America.

What does ring true about this passage is how the American Creed invests everyone who comes here with transcendent value. In this respect, unity is indeed an American sacrament. But it is our pluralism that unites us. Considerable blending has taken place over the years. Nonetheless, the populations that compose the nation are tossed together more than they are blended. America is more like a salad bowl than like a melting pot. Otherwise our motto would be *unum* alone, which decidedly we are not. At our finest, we remain both proudly pluralistic *and* united. When a Russian Jew and a Russian Christian come to America, two things unite them that divided them in the old country: their faith in freedom and their freedom of faith.

William James had employed it a decade earlier to describe American religion, but not until 1915 did the word *pluralism* enter the American political lexicon. The philosopher Horace Kallen (himself a Jewish immigrant) introduced it in his article "Democracy Versus the Melting Pot." Kallen wrote that no alchemist can transform a people's ethnicity into common currency simply by throwing it into a crucible, no matter how society may treasure the notion of universal human coinage. "Men may change their clothes, their politics, their wives, their religions, their philosophies, to a greater or lesser extent, but they cannot change their grandfathers," Kallen wrote. To strike a balance between ethnic and religious uniqueness on the one hand and social cohesion on the other has long been the goal of American pluralism. We forge one larger community out of many smaller ones. We accomplish this, however, not by blending out distinctions but by mutually honoring them.

The metaphor Kallen came up with to describe this form of interdependence is a symphony orchestra. In an orchestra sections complement one another. Varied chords may be struck by different groups of instruments, leading to a rich harmonic texture. The whole is expressive of a strength and complex beauty that could not be simulated by one section of instruments all by itself. "[One] theme shall be dominant, perhaps, among others," Kallen wrote, "but one among many, not the only one." Kallen himself was more committed to plurality than to pluralism. Plurality (or diversity) merely describes a condition; pluralism represents an ideal. In fact, it is *the* American ideal. True to our founders' vision, over the course of the nineteenth century, as America became more diverse our union was strengthened.

No symbol better epitomizes American pluralism than the Statue of Liberty itself. It took nine years for New York City's "first citizens" to raise sufficient money to build a pedestal for it in New York Harbor. One of many unsuccessful fund-raising devices was a portfolio of drawings, letters, and poems contributed by prominent New Yorkers, which the campaign committee collected and put up for auction. It brought in a relative pittance—fifteen hundred dollars. Included in the portfolio was a treasure, however: Emma Lazarus's poem "The New Colossus." Inspired by pogroms against the Jews in Russia, Lazarus celebrated American liberty in words that were selected for the pedestal and unveiled at the dedication ceremony.

> *Not like the brazen giant of Greek fame,*
> *With conquering limbs astride from land to land;*
> *Here at our sea-washed, sunset gates shall stand*
> *A mighty woman with a torch, whose flame*
> *Is the imprisoned lightning, and her name*
> *Mother of Exiles. From her beacon-hand*
> *Glows world-wide welcome; her mild eyes command*
> *The wretched refuse of your teeming shore.*
> *Send these, the homeless, tempest-tossed to me:*
> *I lift my lamp beside the golden door!*

In these few words Lazarus inscribed the Statue of Liberty with American meaning. Its French patrons had offered the statue to commemorate a shared commitment to republican virtue. Conceived as a memorial for Abraham Lincoln in hopes of enhancing Franco-American relations, its original name, "Liberty

Enlightening the World," and its stolid visage were designed to symbolize republican stability not democratic inclusivity. Lazarus's poem transfigured this symbolism, fashioning an image much more emblematic of the American Creed. Rather than glowering at the monarchies of Europe in stately condescension, the Statue of Liberty henceforth welcomed Europe's children to the home of the free.

This embrace did not celebrate anything new about America. The boats had been landing since day one. Walt Whitman, the poet of democracy, wrote in 1882, "All the religions, old and new, are there." But much work remained before American diversity would be elevated to the level of true pluralism. Anticipating the first American centennial and at the twilight of his career, Whitman looked forward to that day when America ("formed from all, with room for all") would fulfill its promise. He dreamt of "a sublime and serious Religious Democracy sternly taking command, dissolving the old, sloughing off surfaces, and from its own interior and vital principles, reconstructing, democratizing society."

What could power such a hope—uniting men and women, rich and poor, people of all races and every faith? Only the founders' vision of *E pluribus unum*. The architects of America—themselves on a holy mission—designed our house (reminiscent of the Lord's house in the Bible) to contain many mansions.

7

AMERICA'S MISSION

Your mission is to improve the state of the world, to
be the "model republic," to show that men are capable of governing themselves, and that the simple and
natural form of government is that also which confers
most happiness on all, is productive of the greatest
development of the intellectual faculties, above all,
that which is attended with the highest standard of
private and political virtue and morality.

—*Albert Gallatin,*
Peace with Mexico, 1847

WHEN THE AMERICAN DIPLOMAT ALBERT GALLATIN SPOKE OUT
against the Mexican War, he was also raising moral concerns
with regard to the newly coined notion of American Manifest
Destiny. From the outset Americans had been on a mission. The
first settlers came to this country on a quest for religious liberty.
The founders sought political liberty, establishing their mission
on a spiritual foundation. Westward expansion—to which John
L. Sullivan gave the appellation "Manifest Destiny" in 1845—
would complete what many Americans had come to believe was
a providential mission to establish the land of the free across

America. Gallatin's concern was that their zeal for expansion would make America's leaders "abandon the lofty position which your fathers occupied, to substitute for it the political morality and heathen patriotism of the heroes and statesmen of antiquity."

The tension between American mission and American imperialism became sharper five decades later near the turn of what would rightly be called the American century. With the continent colonized and international vistas beckoning, the nation's virtues and interests both complemented and contested each other on a larger stage. When our leaders remembered Galletin's warning, the nation was capable of exerting, in his words, "a moral influence most beneficial to mankind at large." Left to its own self-interest, however, freedom's urgings could became strident, even ugly. That the ugly American has so frequently been our caricature abroad is but another indication of how far the nation, when unmindful of its creed, can stray from its own path.

Whatever its expression, whether noble or mean, American mission almost always assumes a high moral tone. This tone is captured as readily by the trumpets of imperialism (disguising the desire to have our way in the world with the rhetoric of freedom) as by voices lifted in international witness to the longstanding American covenant with liberty, equality, and human rights. In both cases, however, that we should testify to our values beyond the nation's borders is a natural extension of America's moral self-image.

On June 2, 1870, appealing to women throughout the world, Julia Ward Howe invented Mother's Day. In a proclamation distributed throughout America and Europe, she called on "all women who have hearts, whether your baptism be of water or of tears," to say firmly: "From the bosom of the devastated earth a voice goes up with our own. It says, 'Disarm, Disarm! The sword of murder is not the balance of justice.' "

It may be hard to imagine the same person who wrote "The Battle Hymn of the Republic" establishing Mother's Day as a platform for women to witness for peace. But in Howe's day many abolitionists were at heart pacifists. Hating slavery more than they despised violence, they chose the Civil War as an exception to the rule. Director of the Perkins School for the Blind in Boston and founder of the Association for the Advancement of Women, Howe was a tireless social activist. Among other things she cofounded was the American Woman Suffrage Association. In 1869 she gave her heart to yet another cause. Responding to the horrors of the Franco-Prussian War, Howe emerged as one of the earliest and most articulate advocates for world peace.

Pointedly, she did not call her annual festival International Peace Day—she called it Mother's Day, knowing of no other group that could more naturally or persuasively sponsor an annual festival in support of love and nonviolence. The object was not to put mothers on a pedestal. She wanted instead to draw mothers out of their kitchens and parlors and into the public square, to unite as many women as she could in a common cause: the protection of children from the threat of war. Or, as she put it, "to promote the alliance of the different nationalities, the amicable settlement of international questions, the great and general interests of peace."

Linking motherhood to disarmament, Howe asserted that the unconditional love they feel for their children invests mothers with a natural and deep interest in preventing bloodshed. On the first Mother's Day, Howe proclaimed, "Let women now leave all that may be left of home for a great and earnest day of counsel. Let them meet first, as women, to bewail and commemorate the dead. Let them then solemnly take counsel with each other as to the means whereby the great human family can live in peace, each bearing after his own time the sacred impress, not of Caesar, but of God." For several years in New York, Boston, and Philadelphia—also in England, Scotland, and Switzerland—peace activists celebrated Mother's Day in Howe's pacific spirit.

By the 1890s, however, the national mood had changed. Over the final quarter of the nineteenth century, the United States had become a world economic and military power. For the first time business (especially banking) interests played a major role in shaping American foreign policy. Multinational corporations emerged. Despite the well-intentioned warnings of our founders not to embroil the nation in international conflicts, it made perfect sense that the United States should begin to play a larger role on the world stage. Moreover, our population wore the world's face, leading the American people to cultivate a natural interest in international affairs. Now that the West was won, new frontiers beckoned. America sought more "elbow room."

The not always gay nineties were as patriotic as they were gilded. Having failed to capture a preoccupied nation's heart, Mother's Day disappeared from the calendar, Flag Day was added, and American citizens began standing for the playing of "The Star-Spangled Banner." Here again, religion contributed to the urgings of patriotism. In fact, American internationalism commenced with American missions; powered by Christian evangelists, international Manifest Destiny led with a prayer book. But over the course of the decade, as our expansionist policies began to meet resistance, the sword grew readier to hand.

The nation's new status as a world power found symbolic expression at the World's Columbian Exposition, which took place in Chicago in 1893 to commemorate the four hundredth anniversary of Columbus's discovery of America. Tens of millions of visitors from around the world came to experience the "alabaster city" erected on Lake Michigan, dreamscape of a confident nation. The Pledge of Allegiance was written for the occasion. Columbus Day became a national holiday. Patriotic curiosities among the fair's 65,000 exhibits were a Liberty Bell fashioned from oranges, a huge map of the nation constructed with pickles, and a Statue of Liberty made of salt. President Grover Cleveland opened the fair by pushing a button that set a mighty gyro whirling and unfurled a giant American flag. Cannons sounded. Church bells rang throughout the city. Ten

thousand voices joined in singing the anthem "America," closing
with its now familiar summation of the American Creed:

> Our fathers' God, to thee,
> Author of liberty,—
>   To thee we sing:
> Long may our land be bright
> With freedom's holy light;
> Protect us by thy might,
>   Great God, our King.

In his address President Cleveland exclaimed, "I cherish the
thought that America stands on the threshold of a great awakening. The impulse with which this Phantom City could rise in
our midst is proof that the spirit is with us." In this international
exhibition Cleveland recognized the national mission. "As by a
touch the machinery that gives life to this vast Exposition is
now set in motion, so at the same instant let our hopes and
aspirations awaken forces which in all time to come shall influence the dignity, and the freedom of mankind." Not all Americans were flush with optimism. John Adams's great-grandson,
the dour and insightful Henry Adams, questioned "whether the
American people knew where they were driving."

Evangelical Christians had little doubt concerning America's
appointed mission; they wondered only whether we would dare
to fulfill our heaven-sent destiny. In 1885, Josiah Strong, a Congregationalist minister, published the first manifesto for American internationalism. His book *Our Country: Its Possible Future
and Its Present Crisis* was an instant bestseller. Its popularity led
to his appointment as general secretary of the Evangelical Alliance, a leading vehicle for social reform and Christian mission.

Strong was not an imperialist, seeking American hegemony
around the globe; he was a missionary who believed that American Protestantism—ecumenical in spirit and practice—was the
perfect catalyst to redeem first the American West and then a
divided world. Born in 1847 and raised in Ohio, he began his
ministry as a missionary in Cheyenne, Wyoming, before return-

ing to his home state to devote himself to charitable work. His second book (*The New Era*, published in 1893) declared the time to be right for an international crusade, one devoted to ameliorating social conditions in conformity with the teachings of the scripture. His goal, through the establishment of international missions, was to nurture the spirit of liberty and equality, foster peace, and enhance security in preparation for the establishment of God's Kingdom.

Americans have long rationalized national and international policies by religious and moral argument. Distant in spirit from the Christian fundamentalism that would emerge thirty years later, Strong's evangelical agenda drew equally from both fonts of American faith: the universalism of the Declaration of Independence and the scriptures themselves. Though wary of Catholicism and Mormonism, Strong—looking first to the nation's westward expansion and then beyond her shores—established his vision for an American world on the basis of civil liberty. Believing the closing years of the nineteenth century to be second in importance only to the time of Christ's incarnation, he pointed to the end of slavery, elevation of women, and an enhanced valuation of human life as the true legacy of Christian faith and American freedom.

Strong viewed American expansionism as a spiritual imperative, not an economic one. Faith demanded that we export the American Creed. This ambition found precedent early in our nation's history. Despite his aversion to international entanglements, Thomas Jefferson himself proclaimed it in a letter he wrote in 1810: "The preservation of the holy fire is confided to us by the world, and the sparks which will emanate from it will ever serve to rekindle it in other quarters of the globe." Though Jefferson believed this kindling would happen by osmosis, American witness to liberty is inherent in the nation's ideals. Eighty years later, this mission took full launch. Noting the spreading dispensation of liberty at home, Strong held up the American Creed as a template for the world's redemption. "Our plea is not America for America's sake," he wrote, "but America for the world's sake. . . . We are the chosen people. We cannot afford to wait. The plans of God will not wait. Those plans seem to have brought us to one of the closing stages in the world's career, in which we can no longer *drift* with safety to our destiny."

As ecumenical as his religious sensibilities were, Strong's Americanism had arch parochial overtones. America's mission was to stamp upon the world not only its values but also Anglo-Saxon culture. As demonstrated by "our rapidly increasing strength in modern times," Strong believed that God was "not only preparing in our Anglo-Saxon civilization the die with which to stamp the people of the earth, but . . . also massing behind that die the mighty power with which to press it." The spirit that informed these words was not as pernicious as their letter. Less a racial bigot than a broad-minded progressive, Strong—however naïve he may have been—was the first of many to shape an international agenda according to the values implicit in American pluralism. Yet, as is often true of American dreamers, his confidence in pluralism was greater than his sensitivity to its intrinsic requirements.

Wedding biblical religion to republican faith, Strong rallied his countrymen to accomplish "the evangelization of the world." This call was answered in two ways: first, by the establishment and rapid growth of an ecumenically sponsored missionary movement; and, second, in the extension of military might beyond the nation's borders. Protestant Christianity and American democracy were exported in the same package. The union of faith and freedom we had established would be promulgated abroad. To accomplish this, if need be, American values would be supported by American arms.

Before World War II, American leaders understood remarkably little about the world beyond our borders. President William McKinley expanded our nation's war with Spain with little justification beyond his stated intention of Christianizing the Philippines, which happened already to be Christian. Yet, as articulated by people such as Strong, the inclusive spirit of America's mission would find expression half a century later in the more universal language of Franklin Delano Roosevelt's Four

Freedoms ("everywhere in the world") and Eleanor Roosevelt's commitment to universal human rights.

Brimful with noble intent, Strong's *Our Country* was among the most influential books of the late 1880s. Albert J. Beveridge's speech "The March of the Flag"—epitomizing Americanism at its worst—takes the same honors a decade later. Among the greatest orators of his time, Beveridge, a young Republican lawyer, delivered his address in Indianapolis's Tomlinson Hall on September 16, 1898. At a time when the Philippine Islands, halfway around the world, could not have been further removed from American consciousness, Beveridge called for the expansion of our fledgling war against Spain to this far-flung Spanish colony. He closed his address with words that cast a long American shadow.

There are so many real things to be done—canals to be dug, railways to be laid, forests to be felled, cities to be builded, fields to be tilled, markets to be won, ships to be launched, peoples to be saved, civilization to be proclaimed, and the flag of liberty flung to the eager air of every sea. Is this an hour to waste upon triflers with nature's laws? Is this a season to give our destiny over to wordmongers and prosperity-wreckers? No! It is an hour to remember our duty to our homes. It is a moment to realize the opportunities fate has opened to us.

Like the Bible, the American script can be adapted for many purposes, noble and ignoble, humble and vain. "Wonderfully has God guided us," Beveridge exclaims. "Yonder at Bunker Hill and Yorktown His providence was above us. At New Orleans and on ensanguined seas His hand sustained us. Abraham Lincoln was His minister and His was the altar of freedom the Nation's soldiers set up on a hundred battle-fields." Such "triflers with nature's laws" as Thomas Jefferson would have cringed. Lincoln would have wondered how his own name and

God's could both be taken so blasphemously in vain.

Beveridge's address epitomizes the idolatry into which American patriotism can easily lapse. Within months of its delivery, 300,000 copies had been distributed across the land. In 1899 it became the centerpiece of many a successful congressional campaign, helping elevate Beveridge himself to the U.S. Senate. Even as Strong's book sounded the keynote for American missions, Beveridge's address was the marching song of American imperialism. The former committed itself to an extension of the nation's values overseas; the latter set out to plant our flag there.

The year 1898 marked a parallel shift in the tenor of the missionary movement. Peaceful witness was augmented by military might. By the time of the First World War, many Christians, including Lyman Abbott (better known for his commitment to the social gospel), considered the war a "twentieth century crusade." That any religious meaning could be wrung out of that conflict demonstrates how quick Americans are to invest their national endeavors with religious significance.

At the risk of their own integrity, religious leaders were increasingly tempted to subjugate their theological principles to the interests of American foreign policy. Shortly after the war ended, to attract converts, the Church of Christ, Scientist, ran a full-page ad in *The New York Times* to proclaim the credo of its founder, Mary Baker Eddy. The order of her statement of beliefs is telling. "I believe strictly in the Monroe Doctrine, in our Constitution, and in the laws of God."

Abraham Lincoln never accepted the proposition that God was on his side. He strove instead to ensure that his actions would place him on the side of God. Others, misinterpreting the letter of the American Creed, show fewer scruples. In times of conflict, rhetoric like that of Albert Beveridge is painfully familiar: "We cannot retreat from any soil where Providence has unfurled our banner; it is ours to save that soil for liberty and civilization." Beveridge and others failed to perceive the irony of suppressing local liberation movements—as in the Philippines—under the name of freedom. American antiimperialists recognized it, however. The philosopher William James wrote, "We are now openly engaged in crushing out the sacredest thing

in this great human world—the attempt of a people long en-
slaved" to win their freedom. At one point 75,000 American
soldiers occupied the Philippines. Entire villages were destroyed
in retaliation for the death of a single American.

President Theodore Roosevelt was foremost among those who
championed a more vigorous United States international presence. In his book *The Strenuous Life* (published in 1900), Roosevelt distilled his rugged Americanism into a bold international
tonic, both intoxicating and dangerous:

> The twentieth century looms before us big with the
> fate of many nations. If we stand idly by, if we seek
> merely swollen, slothful ease and ignoble peace, if we
> shrink from the hard contests where men must win at
> hazard of their lives and at the risk of all they hold
> dear, then the bolder and stronger peoples will pass
> us by, and will win for themselves the domination of
> the world.

Roosevelt closed his term by sending the "Great White Fleet"
around the globe to demonstrate the nation's emergence as a
naval power. He also set the tone for subsequent American foreign adventures, which have always been justified on moral
grounds—pursued for the sake and at the risk of all we hold
dear. Given its stridency, we can be grateful that at the outset
of the twentieth century such moralism had a more lasting impact at home than it did abroad.

If the doctrine of Manifest Destiny rings untrue to the founders'
intentions, in large measure this is because it was inspired as
much by national arrogance as by universal principle. It was not
even embraced by a majority of the American business community. In its early manifestation for most businesses the doctrine offered few immediate prospects for financial gain. But in
other respects the spirit that informed American mission was

nobler than the backlash of American isolationism and protectionism that tends to follow our imperfect forays onto the world
stage. Our power carries with it an attendant responsibility. Our
principles demand witness. If to this extent only, American Manifest Destiny was faithful to the American Creed. In a world
where for many true liberty and democratic pluralism remain
almost unimaginable, we can ill afford the moral luxury of keep-
ing the American dream to ourselves. Whether lamentable, stirring, or both, it is hardly surprising that architects of American
foreign policy should champion their international adventures
with the rhetoric of freedom and faith.

By "speaking softly and carrying a big stick," Theodore Roosevelt presided over peace throughout his presidency. Despite
his bellicose temperament, this remained among the accomplish-
ments of which he was most proud. Roosevelt reveled in war,
glorying in battle and seeing combat as a test of character, yet
he was awarded the Nobel Peace Prize—the first American to
be so honored—for brokering a treaty between Russia and Japan
in 1905. The agreement was signed aboard the presidential yacht
Mayflower in the Long Island Sound.

Though he taught Sunday school during his years at Harvard
and continued faithful in church attendance all his life, Roosevelt
was not a conspicuously religious man. His faith was more ge-
nerically American than specifically denominational. He expressed it by his deeds, not in his words. But he did say this,
in encouraging his fellow Americans to attend church. "[You]
will come away feeling a little more charitably toward all the
world." Whenever we leave church feeling more charitably toward all the world, we walk, at least in part, in step with the
American Creed.

Manifest Destiny was politically naïve and, in many respects,
economically dysfunctional. After an adventure or two (in Cuba,
the Philippines, Panama, and Mexico), it ended in the train
wreck of the First World War. But its goals were not ignoble.
Implicit in the overarching faith sponsored by pluralistic democracy is an evangelical charge. If all people are created equal
and endowed by their Creator with certain inalienable rights,
"all people" represents more than merely the people of the

United States. Josiah Strong and Theodore Roosevelt were in their own fashion as devoted to world peace as Julia Ward Howe was. The late-nineteenth-century transition from American nationalism to a more cosmopolitan and international vision offers a flawed but recognizable template for all future exercise of American power and responsibility in the world.

Responsible power calls itself under judgment. Not alone, this chapter of our history reminds us that patriotism can be as blind as love, for it is a form of love. Searching through my grandparents' attic when I was a boy, I found a handsome wooden plaque picturing a soldier in a broad-brimmed American World War I helmet and embossed in burnished copper with the words "My country, right or wrong." If lifted from its most memorable source, this quote was taken out of context, leaving a misleading impression. What Senator Carl Schurz of Missouri actually said in 1899 was "My country, right or wrong: if right, to be kept right; and if wrong, to be set right." According to the nation's creed, *that* is the American mission.

8

AMERICAN FUNDAMENTALS

The sincere and candid reformer can no longer consider the national Promise as destined to automatic fulfillment. The reformers . . . proclaim their conviction of an indubitable and a beneficent national future. But they do not and cannot believe that this future will take care of itself.

—*Herbert Croly,*
The Promise of American Life, 1909

THE EARLY YEARS OF THE TWENTIETH CENTURY BROUGHT PROfound change. Breakthroughs in travel and communication had drawn disparate peoples together and challenged national identities. World war, world evangelism, and world markets created a discordant yet symphonic challenge to traditional neighborhoods and long-established provincial harmonies. Orchestrated by business and accompanied by science, the relentless march of modernism razed one world as it was creating another.

Modernism sponsored several cognate ideologies: positivism, scientism, rationalism, secularism, liberalism, relativism, evolutionism, and materialism. The ideals of the Enlightenment spurred a growing confidence that by employing reason and by expanding the compass of knowledge human beings could shape their own destiny. By 1900, in Western academic circles this confidence swelled to a near consensus. The natural sciences replaced scripture as the foundation for truth, and soon other disciplines (political science, sociology, psychology, and philosophy) based their authority on the scientific model as well. With religion being relegated to the private arena, it seemed only a matter of time before the old superstitions would fall of their own weight, giving birth to a bright new world, institutionalized in nation-states and free from religious shadows. Religion itself was judged according to scientific (if often pseudoscientific) measurements. Though contested by successive incarnations of Romanticism and Idealism, the world of fact gradually displaced the world of myth in modern consciousness. Its devotions were expressed in many competing forms, but all shared one thing that differentiated modernist ideologies sharply from traditional worldviews. Modernism established and in certain circles attempted to enforce the cult of objectivity.

Though Marxists believed that capitalism was but a stage in human economic development, modernism found in capitalism its most distinctive and enduring economic formulation. Ironically, the early agents of capitalism were deeply religious people. Infused into the world of commerce, the ascetic spirit of Puritanism helped stoke a secular engine that spirited society away from its religious station. In the classic formulation of this irony, *The Protestant Ethic and the Spirit of Capitalism*, the father of modern sociology, Max Weber, mourned what he called "the disenchantment of the world." Entrepreneurial asceticism led citizens of the City of God unconsciously to erect idols to mammon that displaced traditional devotions and eventually removed God from the seat of authority. In Weber's words, "The idea of duty in one's calling prowls around our life like the ghost of dead religious beliefs."

The old gods arose in new form, as avengers, and not only in religious guise. One result of this development was the bloodiest century in the history of the world. At the end of World War I, the Nobel Prize–winning German novelist Hermann Hesse (rediscovered by another generation of spiritual seekers in the 1960s) lamented that this senseless, id-driven conflict "destroyed and lost for the greater part of the civilized world . . . the two universal foundations of life, culture and morality: religion and customary morals." With them was sacrificed the "traditional, sacred, unwritten understanding about what is proper and becoming between people."

Following in the path of this march came unquestionable progress. Looking forward from 1900, thanks to advances in medicine and hygiene, life expectancy in America increased by twenty-nine years in one century. While the gap between rich and poor widened, the quality of life for almost everyone was enhanced. Looking back, most salutary of all were the changes in government first heralded in 1776. Yet progress also proved destabilizing. Fear that modernism was compromising all that is sacred inspired retrenchment. Hence the emergence of fundamentalism.

America is not a Christian nation. It is, however, a religious one. The founders recognized that freedom is a morally neutral quality, defined by the objects to which it is devoted. Without a moral mooring, our liberties run the risk of lapsing into license. When this happens fundamentalists and other people of faith are right to be alarmed. The American Creed doesn't play favorites when it comes to theology—atheists receive the same protections under law that fundamentalists do. It does, however, rest on a moral foundation. To abridge people's religious freedom cuts against the American grain, but no more decisively than to exercise freedom without a sense of moral responsibility. The American Creed calls our nation under the judgment of an authority higher than sect, mammon, or self-interest. Prompted in part by legitimate concerns about the direction society was taking, fundamentalists called on Americans to reopen their Bibles. They insisted that, apart from morality, the country would languish.

American fundamentalism arose during the 1920s, its birth and rapid development a reaction to the ambiguous and amoral energy of modernism. Knowledge invests people with undoubted power, but when the pace of invention outstrips the growth of wisdom, a great deal of knowledge becomes a dangerous thing. Wisdom does advance. The spread of democracy witnesses to that. But, on balance, knowledge alone in no way guarantees that we will be any wiser than St. Paul was. That a Christian should open his or her Bible and discover a compelling indict-ment of modern times is hardly surprising.

The term *fundamentalism* was coined by Curtis Lee Laws in 1920, with the reforms it proposed initially more theological than political in nature. Its foundational documents were a series of pamphlets entitled "The Fundamentals: A Testimony to the Truth," published between 1910 and 1915. These ninety arti-cles (penned by sixty-four writers) laid out the major principles of American fundamentalism: since the Bible is infallible (the literal word of God), one must therefore subscribe to the Virgin Birth, the Resurrection of Christ, Christ's unique atonement for human sin, and the Second Coming.

These theological principles soon found social application. Foremost among fundamentalist concerns was the growing aca-demic consensus around the scientific teaching of evolution. Charles Darwin's *On the Origin of Species by Means of Natural Selection,* written in 1859, posited a long evolutionary ascent from simple to complex organisms driven by the laws and ac-cidents of nature. Not only did this theory contradict the nar-rative of creation outlined in Genesis but it placed biblical authority in jeopardy. In a later book, *The Descent of Man,* Dar-win postulated that human beings are descended from an early family of apes and that chimpanzees, orangutans, and gorillas are our first cousins. This was blasphemy to literal readers of the Bible.

Evolution met its most public challenge in the famous "mon-key trial" in 1925, when John Scopes (a schoolteacher from Dayton, Tennessee) was charged, in effect, with teaching evo-lution to minors. Tennessee had strict laws against the teaching of evolution. In what could have been the most riveting clash of lawyers in our nation's history (had either advocate been per-forming at his peak), America's most famous attorney, Clarence Darrow, hired by the American Civil Liberties Union, spoke for the defense. William Jennings Bryan, three-time Democratic Party nominee for president, led the prosecution. Though Scopes lost his case, these laws were soon overturned, and the final victory went to Darwin. Bryan died days after the trial concluded, and the new order swept onward, lifted on the wings of modernism.

The rapid spread of evolutionary thought fired the fundamentalist crusade with passionate intensity, rallying conservative Christians of many denominations to the cause. The last chapter of Bryan's populist career was devoted to expounding the "Menace of Darwinism," further proof that fundamentalism had become a new populism. To Bryan and many others, the fate of civilization was at stake. Christians who did not rally to the alarm were seen as fellow travelers whose accommodation of the gospel to modernist thought was fast destroying the very foundations of American piety.

Fundamentalism eventually became a political as well as a religious crusade, its uncompromising agenda wreaking havoc on the nation's soul. On its extreme wing, the Ku Klux Klan beat out a racist and anti-Catholic message. This message inverted the stated goal of restoring America to its past honor and integrity. Such extremists swore on their Bibles eternal hostility to the very freedoms to which Jefferson, on the altar of God, had pledged allegiance. Yet other fundamentalist concerns were understandable. As modernism's sails unfurled, moral ballast was needed to steady the nation's course.

In the early twentieth century, radicals on the Christian left were as critical of society as were Christians on the right. The liberal social gospel arose in response to another aspect of modernism, the impact of industrialization on American society. Vast new capital emerged, undisciplined by government regulation. Max Weber wrote, "In the United States, the pursuit of wealth, stripped of its religious and ethical meaning, tends to become associated with purely mundane passions, which often actually give it the character of sport." In these games one side almost always won. With the overwhelming preponderance of new capital filling the endlessly deep pockets of a few robber barons, lacking any governmental gesture in the direction of equity, the proliferation of goods no longer appeared to serve the common good. By 1900 the richest one percent of Americans possessed more property than all other citizens combined. Outrage at this inequity provoked a powerful, and in many ways redemptive, social and religious response.

When Theodore Roosevelt proclaimed, "We stand at Armageddon and battle for the Lord," it was not to inspire his troops to storm San Juan Hill but to launch his reform platform as a Bull Moose candidate for president in 1912. Roosevelt was morally more eloquent in exercising his missionary zeal at home than abroad. Wary of the dangers posed by monopoly capitalism, he pledged the nation's sacred honor to dash "the tyranny of mere wealth, the tyranny of plutocracy." With his Square Deal anticipating his cousin Franklin Delano Roosevelt's New Deal, Theodore Roosevelt raised the platform of American social justice.

Though a Republican, and by no means an enemy of American business, Roosevelt developed a repugnance for the amassing of great wealth. He was also wary of overdevelopment, championing the conservation of natural resources. During the course of his presidency, Roosevelt doubled the national park system, created sixteen national bird refuges, thirteen national forests, fifteen national monuments, and twenty federal irrigation projects. In his domestic policy Roosevelt epitomized the American spirit of social responsibility. As personally upright as any American president, he described his political platform as "fundamentally an ethical movement." At a time when American corporations were poised to take over the country—directing national policy with many fewer restrictions than they operate under today—Roosevelt systematically attacked "the swollen fortunes" and "entrenched privilege" of the "malefactors of great wealth."

The robber barons (as they came to be known) threatened to hijack the nation's soul. Curbing monopolies alone was not enough, however. Spiraling inequalities of wealth imperiled social peace as well as social justice. Over the years Roosevelt's views became more radical. By 1912 he was advocating campaign finance reform and was among the first to propose both an income tax and an inheritance tax. For Roosevelt, a more equitable tax code had as much to do with morals as with economics. Vast fortunes not only threatened the integrity of the social compact but also weakened the moral fiber of families enthralled by their possession. At a time when the American Creed was in danger of being replaced by the god of mammon, Roosevelt was the first president to marshal the full force of the federal government to empower his moral vision.

Pressure for reform had been building for decades. Even before the Civil War, the Congregationalist minister Horace Bushnell (a harbinger of the social gospel movement) had reminded Americans that both Puritan polity and our founders' republican faith put all citizens "on a footing of spiritual equality and fraternity." As a nation we must witness to the world "the power there is in the gospel to establish at once, equality and order, liberty and justice, and so to organize a free commonwealth." Josiah Strong too—even as he called for global witness to American Christian values—had cautioned against the deleterious impact of unbridled selective prosperity upon the nation's soul. He mentioned in particular "the dangers of Mammonism, materialism, luxuriousness, and the centralization of wealth."

"God gave me my money," John D. Rockefeller once said. By him and others of his tiny class, massive charitable tithes were offered as demonstration of this fact. But religious critics didn't view Rockefeller and his cohorts quite so generously. When the untrammeled power of wealth began to supplant government power and undermine social stability, social prophets opened their Bibles and read a very different message. Coupled with Theodore Roosevelt's trust-busting, the spread of the social gospel through the first decade of the twentieth century recalled our nation to higher ground.

The campaign on behalf of America's working poor often expressed itself as a critique of capitalism. One founder of the social gospel movement, the theologian Walter Rauschenbusch, dismissed capitalism as "a mammonistic organization with which Christianity can never be content." The same conviction echoed in American literature and from mainline Christian pulpits. Theodore Dreiser may have lampooned evangelical religion in his novel *An American Tragedy,* yet its hero meets destruction when he rebels against his parents' faith to pursue the God of mammon. Describing the debasement of God into "a sort of magnified Rotarian" worshiped in (what another critic dubbed) the "Saint Carnagie Temple of Positive Christianity," Charles Fiske, an Episcopal bishop from central New York, lamented that "America has become almost hopelessly enamoured of a religion that is little more than a sanctified commercialism; it is hard in this day and in this land to differentiate between religious aspiration and business prosperity."

Ultimately Christian socialists were no more successful than fundamentalists in reconfiguring the American Creed to suit their own ideology. But reactionary and radical alike sounded legitimate warnings of how soft the moral underpinnings of modernism actually were. To a Christian, neither bankbook nor textbook can replace the authority of the Bible.

Uniting the moral urgings of both left and right was William Jennings Bryan. From the 1880s until his death in 1925, Bryan was America's leading populist. A vigorous advocate for women's suffrage and American labor, he feared that Darwin's teachings would "weaken the cause of democracy and strengthen class pride and the power of wealth." His principal concern was not Darwinism proper but the dangers posed by social Darwinism, a loose extrapolation of Darwin's scientific teachings into social policy.

Though committed to protectionism when it served their personal interests, American business leaders trumpeted "the survival of the fittest" to justify unrestricted competition. The social Darwinist William Graham Sumner coupled evolution with progress in the most un-American terms imaginable. "Let it be understood that we cannot go outside of this alternative: liberty, inequality, survival of the fittest; not-liberty, equality, survival of the unfittest. The former carries society forward and favors all its best members; the latter carries society downwards and favors all its worst members." In response, Bryan opened both his Bible and his Declaration of Independence. Condemning the economic blasphemy of a cross of gold while attacking the liberties taken by American moguls at the people's expense, he proclaimed, "Man is the handiwork of God and was placed upon earth to carry out a Divine purpose. The corporation is the handiwork of man and was created to carry out a money-making policy. . . . Man acts under the restraints of conscience. . . . A corporation has no soul."

On his way to Tennessee to prosecute the Scopes trail, Bryan paid a visit to Monticello, Thomas Jefferson's home. The irony of this pilgrimage apparently escaped him. Yet in one respect Bryan was as true to the American Creed as his hero. No American faithful to the founders' vision can view social outcomes as independent of moral consequence. Despite the shoddiness of his science and the questionable nature of his economic policies, Bryan recognized that conscience is the handmaiden of American freedom. Conscience also touches the heart of what it means to be human. This argument can be made from the left or right. Freedom and conscience are both sacrificed when freedom is exercised without consulting conscience's oracle. All that remains is a social Darwinist swamp, with the Devil taking the hindmost.

So strongly established is the American Creed in American hearts that fundamentalist crusades and radical social movements succeed only insofar as they remain true to the original spirit of the founders. The development of our legal code and juridical reinterpretation of the Constitution reflect the impact of such movements, but never finally at the expense of the broad covenant that unites us as a people. In social policy we will opt for fairness, especially on liberty's behalf, but only to the extent that other basic liberties are not sacrificed on equity's altar. To give but one example, Upton Sinclair wrote The Jungle as a paean to socialism. As such, it failed to convert its audience. Yet the horrors of factory conditions that Sinclair depicted led to the establishment of the federal Food and Drug Administration. The same holds true for religion. In religion Americans are willing to accept absolutes for themselves. Ultimately, however, we have proved unwilling (at least for long) to impose our absolutes on others.

The founders themselves were neither religious fundamentalists nor economic radicals. Nonetheless, they established in the American Creed a set of fundamentals that would remain the bearing point for succeeding generations, and serve as an instrument for those who would reform the nation's course. Even as religious liberals and evangelicals combined to lead the campaign for abolition in the early nineteenth century, it is no accident that decades later religious champions from both right and left would, in their respective ways, call the amoral impulse of modernism under judgment. Extremism on behalf of liberty (or justice) can be a vice, violating the balance struck by the founders. But by raising moral issues at a time of national drift (or overdrive), given the self-correcting gyro of our covenant, reformers almost always serve the broader purposes of the American Creed. American fundamentals and American fundamentalism (whether of the right or left) are very different things, but the former makes room for the latter. Especially at times of moral degeneration or spiritual crisis, by paying heed to both reactionary and radical admonitions the nation can correct its course.

9

THE FOUR FREEDOMS

Just as our national policy in internal affairs has been based upon a decent respect for the rights and dignity of all our fellowmen within our gates, so our national policy in foreign affairs has been based on a decent respect for the rights and dignity of all nations, large and small. And the justice of morality must and will win in the end.

—*Franklin Delano Roosevelt,*
Annual Message to Congress,
January 6, 1941

In his famous Four Freedoms address to Congress, Franklin Roosevelt also said, "This nation has placed its destiny in the hands and heads and hearts of its millions of free men and women; and its faith in freedom under the guidance of God. Freedom means the supremacy of human rights everywhere. Our support goes to those who struggle to gain those rights or keep them." As did many of his predecessors, Roosevelt professed an encompassing faith. Through much of his adult life he served as head warden of St. James' Church in Hyde Park, New York. His parents were married at the church I serve, All Souls Unitarian in Manhattan. The Four Freedoms address finds its moral grounding in both Christian ethics and the founders' vision.

Stating that "there is nothing mysterious about the foundations of a healthy and strong democracy," Roosevelt claimed that the basic things Americans expect from their government are simple: "Equality of opportunity for youth and for others; jobs for those who can work; security for those who need it; the ending of special privilege for the few; the preservation of civil liberties for all; the enjoyment of the fruits of scientific progress in a wider and constantly rising standard of living." With the exception of guaranteed jobs and an ever-expanding prosperity, each of these things falls squarely within the purview of the American Creed. "The inner and abiding strength of our economic and political systems is dependent upon the degree to which they fulfill these expectations," Roosevelt said.

He added the most memorable part of his speech at the last moment, in his seventh draft. It proclaims a global vision based on the establishment of four essential freedoms:

> The first is freedom of speech and expression—everywhere in the world. The second is freedom of every person to worship God in his own way—everywhere in the world. The third is freedom from want—which, translated into world terms, means economic understandings which will secure to every nation a healthy peacetime life for its inhabitants—everywhere in the world. The fourth is freedom from fear—which, translated into world terms, means a worldwide reduction of armaments to such a point and in such a thorough fashion that no nation will be in a position to commit an act of physical aggression against any neighbor—everywhere in the world.

When Roosevelt finished dictating this passage, he invited comments from the staff members present in the Oval Office. Harry Hopkins, one of the president's principal advisers, questioned the phrase "everywhere in the world." "That covers an awful lot of territory, Mr. President," he said. "I don't know how interested Americans are going to be in the people of Java." Roosevelt's reply proved prescient. "I'm afraid they'll have to be someday, Harry. The world is getting so small that even the people in Java are getting to be our neighbors now."

The file of clippings Roosevelt consulted as he was writing this speech contains two sources for his lists of six foundations and four freedoms. The first is a quotation from an economic bill of rights circulating in England, setting international minimum standards for housing, food, education, and medical care, along with free speech, free press, and freedom of worship. The second is a list of five proposals offered in an unprecedented ecumenical statement by Catholic and Protestant leaders in England. These included the abolition of extreme inequalities of wealth; equal opportunity of education, regardless of class or race; protection for the family; restoration of a sense of divine vocation to daily work; and all the earth's resources dedicated to the benefit of the whole human race. His detractors' views aside, Roosevelt's platform was progressive not socialist. He sought not to abolish but only to temper extreme inequalities of wealth. Yet he certainly embraced the spirit of these proposals. By so doing he advanced the pragmatic idealism of the nation's founders.

Roosevelt's speech illustrates the difference between so-called negative freedoms and positive freedoms. For negative freedoms (freedom from abuse, oppression, cruelty—violations of person or property) to be protected, government need only ensure that an individual's person or property be in no way trespassed without penalty. Adam Smith said that the laws of justice are most frequently observed when we mind our own business. But he went on to insist that a person who merely *observes* the laws of justice has little moral merit. A society established on negative rights alone would be both unloving and unlovely. Yet without such rights a free society would be impossible. In and of themselves, negative freedoms presuppose a degree of ethical commitment by demanding reciprocal respect.

Positive freedoms are more clearly bound to ethical obligation. The freedoms of speech and religious liberty represent something more than rights necessary for protection and security. They express liberty *to*, not liberty *from*. Following the letter of American scripture, Roosevelt proclaimed such freedoms and their attendant obligations to be full human rights, fulfilling the promise of our humanity. Without an innate grounding in the law of nature, positive freedoms would be rhetorical only. To Roosevelt they were bedrock—chapter and verse of the American Creed.

That Franklin Roosevelt's policies should have appeared radical at the time is not surprising. His predecessors had wandered far from the founders' faith. Calvin Coolidge summed up his own version of America's creed in six words: "The business of America is business." Though far more progressive than Coolidge, Herbert Hoover elaborated on this sentiment: "The function of government is to bring about a condition of affairs favorable to the beneficial development of private enterprise." Roosevelt viewed America as a "concert of interests" or a "community of interest." Each part of society "must think of itself as a part of a greater whole: one piece in a large design." Attacking those who held that, in America, aside from God only business was sacred, Roosevelt fulminated, "They steal the livery of great national constitutional ideals to serve discredited special interests."

When Roosevelt said "The only thing we have to fear is fear itself," he was speaking not of war but of the Great Depression. In 1929 the stock market crashed, triggering economic panic. The gross national product fell by a third. Thousands of Americans stood in soup lines. Shantytowns had sprung up in America's great cities. A quarter of the workforce could not find a job. American farmers were devastated, many having lost everything, including their land. Roosevelt's inspiration for these famous words came in part during worship at St. James' Church the Sunday before. "This is a day of consecration," he wrote in pencil at the top of his printed manuscript. As great leaders do in times of crisis, he perceived opportunity amid the danger:

"The money changers have fled from their high seats in the temple of our civilization. We may now restore that temple to the ancient truths."

Over the next one hundred days, Roosevelt enacted a set of economic reforms more sweeping than any we have witnessed before or since in our nation's history. He reopened the banks, set up the Tennessee Valley Authority and the Civilian Conservation Corps, established a safety net for farmers and small investors—in all, he proposed and signed into law fifteen major bills. Greater changes, including the Social Security Act of 1935, were to follow. "With the clear consciousness of seeking old and precious moral values" (as he himself put it), Roosevelt reinvented America.

As Abraham Lincoln had done before him, Roosevelt grounded his political philosophy in the Declaration of Independence. In his Commonwealth Club Address (delivered during his campaign against Hoover), he said:

The final term of the high contract was for liberty and the pursuit of happiness. We have learned a great deal of both in the past century. We know that individual liberty and individual happiness mean nothing unless both are ordered in the sense that one man's meat is not another man's poison.

Faith in America, faith in our tradition of personal responsibility, faith in our institutions, faith in ourselves demand that we recognize the new terms of the old social contract. We shall fulfill them, as we fulfilled the obligation of the apparent utopia which Jefferson imagined for us in 1776 and which Jefferson, Roosevelt, and Wilson sought to bring to realization. We must do so, lest a rising tide of misery, engendered by our common failure, engulf us all. But failure is not an American habit; and in the strength of great hope we must all shoulder our common load.

Roosevelt invoked the examples of Thomas Jefferson, Theodore Roosevelt, and Woodrow Wilson often in his speeches. For
the clarity with which they articulated the American Creed,
these three presidents (together with Abraham Lincoln, to whom
Roosevelt turned for inspiration as war grew imminent) stood
preeminent among his predecessors. Jefferson's Declaration of Independence established our national faith. The other two were
both, in their ways, personal mentors.

Family ties connected the two Roosevelts. Theodore was not
only Franklin's cousin but also Eleanor Roosevelt's uncle. When
Franklin and Eleanor married in 1905, Uncle Teddy (then president) gave the bride away. The two followed remarkably similar career paths. Both served in the New York legislature and
as governor of that state; both were assistant secretary of the
navy; and both were selected as vice presidential running mates
before becoming president. They were equally akin in their devotion and fidelity to the American Creed.

In 1912, making a bid to recapture the presidency, Theodore
Roosevelt was defeated by Woodrow Wilson. Before Jimmy Carter took office, Wilson was perhaps the most devout of our nation's presidents. The son of a Presbyterian minister, he was
born again at the age of seventeen—an experience he called the
most important in his life. Wilson had significant moral blind
spots—integration was set back during his presidency and he
showed callous disregard for the rights of African American citizens. He could speak without affectation about a "nation under
God" while failing to capture the nation's essence. Yet, if at
times his pious rhetoric overreached or missed the mark, in international affairs his faith in God and America combined to
express high moral purpose.

Believing America to be "the great idealistic force of history,"
Wilson viewed our mission in evangelistic terms. "I, for one,
believe more profoundly than in anything else human in the
destiny of the United States. I believe that she has a spiritual
energy in her which no other nation can contribute to the liberation of mankind." At the end of World War I, sailing across
the Atlantic to take part in the peace conference, Wilson said of

America, "We are to be an instrument in the hands of God to see that liberty is made secure for mankind."

Presenting the peace treaty to the U.S. Senate for ratification, Wilson looked forward to fulfilling this dream by establishing a League of Nations. In the new world he envisioned, the American dream would become an international reality.

> The stage is set, the destiny is disclosed. It has come about by no plan of our conceiving, but by the hand of God who led us into this way. We cannot turn back. We can only go forward, with lifted eyes and freshened spirit, to follow the vision. It was of this that we dreamed at our birth. America shall in truth show the way. The light streams on the path ahead, and nowhere else.

As often is the case with patriotic piety, one longs here for a dose of Abraham Lincoln's dour theological realism. Others were quick to offer something like it. In 1920, observing how unresponsive the people of America and Europe were to Wilson's preaching, one advocate for the League of Nations noted, "The so-called Christian nations are approaching moral and spiritual bankruptcy as is clearly revealed by the apathy of public opinion on the great moral issues which underlie the Treaty and the League." As is true today, many Americans then were wary of international conventions that might impose unwanted obligations on our nation or its people. Senator Henry Cabot Lodge of Massachusetts warned prudently against trying "to establish a monopoly of idealism." We should attend to America first, he argued. We have our own problems. "We would not have our country's vigor exhausted or her moral force abated, by everlasting meddling and muddling in every quarrel, great and small, which afflicts the world." From that day forward the American pendulum would swing from isolationism to interventionism. We would err in an excess of each.

The American clergy too were divided over the League of

Nations. Some ministers were wary of all foreign entanglements. Even those who viewed America's world mission as providential had their doubts. According to Wilson's design, small nations would garner disproportionate influence in such a league. More worrisome to many ministers was the concern expressed by Edward Conwell, a Baptist pulpiteer from Philadelphia. Conwell was opposed to America joining purposes with the Islamic nations. Taking as his text words from St. Paul—"Do not be mismated with unbelievers. For what partnership have righteousness and iniquity?"—he asked, "Shall we join a League of Nations and go into a partnership with Turkey with all their extreme ferocities?"

Many of the Fourteen Points on which Wilson based his blueprint were difficult to effect. He was crippled by a stroke during the final year of his presidency. And his refusal to compromise destroyed all chances for a League. Nearly thirty years would pass before a version of Wilson's dream would become a reality with the creation of the United Nations. Nonetheless, by announcing a vision of one world, where amity would be established according to the ideals of liberty and justice for all, Wilson gave wider voice to the American Creed. In his paraphrase of Jefferson's Declaration, Wilson declared American principle to be "the principle of justice to all peoples and nationalities, and their right to live on equal terms of liberty and safety with one another, whether they be strong or weak."

In President Wilson's failed attempt, and later as articulated by Franklin Roosevelt, as the twentieth century progressed America became more clearly identified with a global vision. Eleanor Roosevelt played a significant role advancing this vision when, as chair of the Human Rights Commission of the new United Nations, she helped author the Universal Declaration of Human Rights. For her the United Nations represented "the greatest hope for a peaceful world." Looking to the future, she declared, "We must use all the knowledge we possess—all the avenues for seeking agreement and international understanding—not only for our own good, but for the good of all human beings."

The Universal Declaration as adopted by the United Nations General Assembly on December 10, 1948, echoes Jefferson's words in the Declaration of Independence. All people are equally "endowed with reason and conscience," it states. "The inherent dignity and the equal and inalienable rights of all members of the human family is the foundation for freedom, justice, and peace in the world." Franklin Roosevelt's Four Freedoms are present as well: "Human beings shall enjoy freedom of speech and belief and freedom from fear and want." Here too, as with the American Declaration, without an innate foundation establishing human liberty and equality on universal grounds, terms such as "inalienable rights" and "fundamental rights" (employed later in the universal declaration) reduce to oxymorons.

When the universal declaration was presented to the General Assembly, the four Moslem delegates abstained. Religious freedom was contrary to the teachings of the Qur'an, they argued. The foreign minister of Pakistan, Sir Zafrulla Khan, disagreed. "It is my opinion that our Pakistan delegate has misinterpreted the Qur'an. I understand the Qur'an to say: 'He who can believe shall believe; he who cannot believe shall disbelieve; the only unforgiveable sin is to be a hypocrite.' I shall vote for acceptance of the Universal Declaration of Human Rights." When the final roll was called, no country voted to reject the declaration. Russia, Saudi Arabia, and South Africa abstained. In an abiding irony, the U.S. Senate has never ratified the Universal Declaration of Human Rights, suggesting that the Declaration of Independence might itself be controversial were it to be proposed today.

Eleanor Roosevelt centered her practical faith on the second great commandment, to love thy neighbor. "Denominations mean little to me," she said in an interview shortly before she died. "If we pattern our lives on the life of Christ—and sincerely try to follow his creed of compassion and love as expressed in the Sermon on the Mount—we will find that sectarianism means less and less. . . . To me, the way your personal religion makes you live is the only thing that really matters." Her favorite passage in the Bible was 1 Corinthians 13:

"Now abideth faith, hope, charity, these three, but the greatest of these is charity."

Hardheaded pundits argue that one cannot cobble together a program for society on the basis of charity, compassion, and neighborliness. "The Sermon on the Mount is the last word in Christian ethics," Winston Churchill said. "Still, it is not on those terms that Ministers assume their responsibilities of guiding states." Though neighborly love is routinely dismissed by statesmen as hopeless idealism, one cannot help but ponder the point Franklin Roosevelt made to Harry Hopkins. The world is changing; the globe, shrinking. As they do, the old idealism gradually becomes a new realism. Neighborly love may not always prove possible in the international arena, but neighborliness is today less a moral luxury than a requirement for survival. Only one president, Jimmy Carter, has made human rights the centerpiece of his foreign policy. Yet, more than any other, this ideal speaks from the heart of the American Creed.

In 1941 the Jefferson Memorial Commission submitted proposed wording from the Declaration of Independence to be engraved in marble on one of the panels at the new memorial built in Jefferson's memory next to the Tidal Basin near the Washington Mall. Because there was room for only 325 letters on any given panel, the document had to be foreshortened dramatically. Dissatisfied that certain favorite words had been omitted in the edit, Franklin Roosevelt tried his hand at reducing the Declaration to its very essence and recommended passages that he felt must be included. Taking a few small liberties with the text, the committee obliged.

WE HOLD THESE TRUTHS TO BE SELF-EVIDENT: THAT ALL MEN ARE CREATED EQUAL, THAT THEY ARE ENDOWED BY THEIR CREATOR WITH CERTAIN INALIENABLE RIGHTS, AMONG THESE ARE LIFE, LIBERTY

AND THE PURSUIT OF HAPPINESS, THAT TO
SECURE THESE RIGHTS GOVERNMENTS ARE
INSTITUTED AMONG MEN. WE . . . SOLEMNLY
PUBLISH AND DECLARE, THAT THESE COLO-
NIES ARE AND OF RIGHT OUGHT TO BE FREE
AND INDEPENDENT STATES. . . . AND FOR
THE SUPPORT OF THIS DECLARATION, WITH
A FIRM RELIANCE ON THE PROTECTION OF
DIVINE PROVIDENCE, WE MUTUALLY PLEDGE
OUR LIVES, OUR FORTUNES AND OUR SA-
CRED HONOUR.

Missing in the Commission's first draft, the final line was
added at Roosevelt's behest. Jefferson had closed the Declaration
with a ringing peroration, reprising the language of the preamble. To support their claims to life, liberty, and the pursuit of
happiness (rights bestowed by nature's God), the founders
pledged their lives, fortunes, and sacred honor (relying on God's
protection). These final instructions were not lost on either
Franklin or Eleanor Roosevelt. Both devoted their public lives
to liberty and justice for all, here at home and everywhere in
the world.

In a speech he was drafting during the week before his death
in April 1945, Franklin wrote, "Today we are faced with the
preeminent fact that, if civilization is to survive, we must cultivate the science of human relationships—the ability of all peoples, of all kinds, to live together and work together, in the same
world, at peace." Shortly before her own death, when pondering the same difficulties, Eleanor expressed her conviction that,
with due sacrifice, we will succeed in rekindling our nation's
light. "In the past, we have never failed to meet any challenge
or threat which confronted us. In the future, I am confident we
will master this too, but we must use the full resources of our
faith in order to prevail."

Given the dangers we face, the founders' ideals are more
important today than ever. For this reason, we would do well

to heed Eleanor Roosevelt's prudent counsel. "It is high time that we Americans took a good look at ourselves, . . . remembering how we established a land of freedom and democracy, remembering what we believed in when we did it."

10

New Frontiers, Old Truths

The rights of man come not from the generosity of the
state, but from the hand of God.

> —*John F. Kennedy,*
> *Inaugural Address,*
> *January 20, 1961*

Speaking to the Georgetown University Alumni Association
in the fall of 1948, Father John Tracy Ellis, a church historian
from Catholic University, expressed apprehension about the future of the United States. His concern—the growing number of
Americans professing their faith in what he called "the cult of
democracy." To make his meaning clear, Ellis quoted General
Dwight D. Eisenhower. On the day he became president of Columbia University, Eisenhower said, "I am the most intensely
religious man I know. Nobody goes through six years of war
without faith. That doesn't mean I adhere to any sect. A democracy cannot exist without a religious base. I believe in democracy."

General Eisenhower was not among our country's most articulate leaders. Shortly after his election to the presidency he
said, "Our government makes no sense unless it is founded in
a deeply felt religious faith, and I don't care what it is." One
can understand why those who didn't criticize Eisenhower for
making such statements seized the opportunity to ridicule him

for them. Yet he was true to his American heritage when linking faith to freedom in the way he often did. It is certainly preferable that an American soon to become president should profess a belief in democracy rather than a belief in business. Near the end of his first term, in words that could not be misconstrued, Eisenhower spoke again on the subject. "Recognition of the Supreme Being is the first, the most basic expression of Americanism," he said. "Without God, there could be no American form of government, nor an American way of life."

Eisenhower's comments about religion and democracy contain something to offend almost everyone. On the one hand, he appears religiously indifferent. On the other, he invests our government with God's mantle. His thought is difficult to parse, but—save for his exclusion of atheists from the national mosaic—each of the statements just quoted is congruous with the American Creed. By linking faith to freedom, Eisenhower was echoing a refrain first sounded in the Declaration of Independence. The propositions upon which the nation is founded *are* propositions of faith. And it *doesn't* matter what specific religion the American people embrace (or even that individual Americans profess no religion), for those propositions affirm religious pluralism and protect religious liberty.

Yet Ellis was right in warning against a cult of democracy. In the 1950s, American civil religion was shallow, undemanding, and unself-critical. It lacked the moral fiber of Benjamin Franklin's "public faith," the universal principles of which were intended to infuse society with a strong civil ethic conducive to the common good. Eisenhower recited the American Creed by rote. "I believe that faith in God and the Judaeo-Christian ethic inspired the Founding Fathers of the United States," he said. "We are a religious nation today because in the Declaration of Independence they stated their full reliance on 'the laws of nature and nature's God' and because they published before the world these self-evident truths." The letter is perfect, but the spirit was missing.

Typical of American religion in the fifties, civil religion during the Eisenhower years was more comforting than prophetic. Eisenhower himself soft-pedaled three of the great moral issues of the time: nuclear proliferation, racial justice, and McCarthyism. Yet, at the very end of his presidency, in his remarkable Farewell Address, he brought the highest American values directly to bear on public policy. Warning against "the acquisition of unwarranted influence . . . by the military-industrial complex," he challenged two of the principal shibboleths of American modernism.

The stockpile of nuclear armaments grew twentyfold between 1952 and 1960. Dedicated to a nonintrusive presidency, Eisenhower did little to stem the tide of peacetime military expansion yet remained wary of it. In 1954 he employed words like *crazy* and *unconscionable* to describe the nation's nuclear buildup. In 1960 he expressed "disgust" that we were producing four hundred Minuteman missiles a year.

Eisenhower was equally laissez-faire in confronting the American industrial complex. During the 1950s, free enterprise became a creed in itself, one sufficient to power the financial engines of America, but threatening to the nation's soul. Though an enthusiast of untrammeled free enterprise, even before his Farewell Address Eisenhower appears to have recognized the connection between arms production and business interests. "Obviously something besides the strict military needs of this country is coming to influence decisions," he admitted in an early news conference. On leaving office he was more explicit in his warnings concerning the collusion of business interests and military expansion. Since he was not only our president but also the nation's most honored soldier, his Farewell Address rang with as much authority as it evoked surprise.

> The conjunction of an immense military establishment and a large arms industry is new in the American experience. The total influence—economic, political, even spiritual—is felt in every city, every statehouse, every office of the federal government. . . . We must never let the weight of this combination endanger our liberties or democratic processes. We should take nothing for granted. Only an alert and knowledgeable

citizenry can compel the proper meshing of the huge
industrial and military machinery of defense with our
peaceful methods and goals so that security and liberty
may prosper together.

Eisenhower viewed the unfettered spread of the military-
industrial complex as a spiritual as well as political problem.
People, not corporations, are invested with inherent worth and
dignity. When the marketplace drives American policy, we can
lose our sense of moral direction. Though he was far from being
forceful in shaping policy that might facilitate his moral ideals,
Eisenhower remained concerned that a materialist value system
would weaken the American character. He feared that, fixated
on the multiplication and distribution of goods, we might lose
sight of the good itself.

In 1954, during Eisenhower's first term, the words *under God*
were added to the Pledge of Alliance. That same year Senator
Joseph McCarthy was at the height of his influence, chairing the
decidedly anti-American Senate Un-American Activities Committee. Two years later, "In God we trust" officially became the
national motto. The words had been in the public domain for
years. Half a century earlier, in 1908, when American monopolies were yet to be broken, Congress had authorized them to
be minted on all gold and silver coinage. (Theodore Roosevelt
opposed the legislation.) Given the prejudices of those who sponsored the respective bills, these congressional actions could easily
be viewed as pernicious, hypocritical, or both. If "In God we
trust" is taken to indicate divine approval rather than suggesting
the highest standard for behavior, it is clearly idolatrous.

Abraham Lincoln—for whom trust in any power less than
divine smacked of self-righteousness—understood the nation's
motto as a moral benchmark. He approved its first use on coinage
with the introduction of the two-cent piece in 1864. Not incon-
gruously, given Jefferson's language in the Declaration of Independence, it was later engraved on the Jefferson nickel from its
inception in 1938. Nonetheless, slogans like "One nation under
God" and "In God we trust" understandably make First Amend-

ment advocates nervous. Only if we interpret them by the light of the American Creed are they worthy expressions of the national spirit. So understood, we are a nation "under God," not over God. We place our trust in a higher judge and power, not any lesser idol erected in the name of commerce or military might.

Eisenhower began every cabinet meeting with a moment of silent prayer. Some Americans, both religious and irreligious, are wary of such intrusions of religion into statecraft. But in this respect Eisenhower was faithful to American tradition. On his final presidential appearance, he even added a memorable footnote to it. He closed his Farewell Address with a prayer that, as an expression of the American Creed, has no equal in twentieth-century presidential literature.

> We pray that peoples of all faiths, all races, all nations may have their great human needs satisfied, that those now denied opportunity shall come to enjoy it to the full; that all who yearn for freedom may experience its spiritual blessings; that those who have freedom will understand, also, its heavy responsibilities; that all who are insensitive to the needs of others will learn charity; that the scourges of poverty, disease and ignorance will be made to disappear from the earth, and that, in the goodness of time, all peoples will come to live together in a peace guaranteed by the binding force of mutual respect and love.

Spoken within three days of one another, Eisenhower's Farewell Address and John F. Kennedy's Inaugural Address serve as bookends for the American Creed. Kennedy appealed to the American moral imagination with eloquence worthy of his greatest forebears. That Kennedy should keynote his presidency with explicit theological language was surprising, however. He was less devout in his personal professions of faith than his predecessor had been. And the religious attacks leveled against him during the campaign on account of his Catholicism might easily have led him to shy from anything more than the customary nod in God's direction when addressing the American people for the first time as their president.

The attacks on Kennedy's Roman Catholicism had been fierce. I remember receiving quarters in change with a red cardinal's cap drawn in Magic Marker on George Washington's head. "What seemed to me most deplorable," Eleanor Roosevelt lamented, "was not the fact that so many people feared the strength of the Roman Catholic Church; it was that they had no faith in the strength of their own way of life and their own Constitution."

Entering the lists against Kennedy was no less a public religious icon than Norman Vincent Peale. Peale broke his political neutrality in founding Citizens for Religious Freedom, made up of evangelical Christian ministers convinced that, if elected, Kennedy would mortgage America to the Vatican. His blessing proved so respected an imprimatur that anti-Catholic bigotry began to be voiced more openly. Peale was shaken by the passions he had helped to unleash and publicly repudiated his own organization. But the damage had been done. Forty years later the Kennedy speechwriter Theodore Sorensen noted how ironic it is that the denominational heirs to those who expressed concern that Kennedy's religious views would influence his political decisions "now openly and expressly urge that their religious doctrines be favored over others, that their members in office set public policies according to those religious doctrines, and that their political views be binding on their congregations."

In his Inaugural Address, Kennedy affirmed the divine foundation of our highest principles by calling the nation under judgment. Placed together, the opening and closing passages of his address update the creed of the founders to address the challenges of a new age. I was present that frigid winter morning. The ringing rhetoric I admired then has lost nothing over the passing years. Sorensen drafted the speech. Adlai Stevenson, Walter Lippmann, John Kenneth Galbraith, and others contributed their thoughts. Today the words best remembered from Kennedy's address are "Ask not what your country can do for you—ask

what you can do for your country." These words inspire patriotic goose bumps to this very day. What people may have forgotten is that Kennedy placed this exhortation in a clear
theological light, one more familiar perhaps to his most revered
presidential predecessors than to a majority of the pundits who
exegete such pronouncements.

> We observe today not a victory of party but a cele-
> bration of freedom—symbolizing an end as well as a
> beginning—signifying renewal as well as change. For
> I have sworn before you and Almighty God the same
> solemn oath our forebears prescribed nearly a century
> and three-quarters ago.

> The world is very different now. For man holds in
> his mortal hands the power to abolish all forms of
> human poverty and all forms of human life. And yet
> the same revolutionary beliefs for which our forebears
> fought are still at issue around the globe—the belief
> that the rights of man come not from the generosity
> of the state but from the hand of God.

Opening his address in this manner, Kennedy followed the
letter of our Declaration of Independence. Since liberty is a divine, innate bequest, promised alike to all of God's children, its
irresponsible exercise betrays our inheritance. In Kennedy's
words, "to abolish all forms of human poverty" is to act according to the highest urgings of our nature; "to abolish . . . all forms
of human life" is to exercise our God-given liberty in the most
godless way imaginable. Only by embracing the moral responsibilities attendant to liberty can we employ our freedom (as the
founders intended) to enhance the common good.

By taking liberties with our freedom, we place ourselves under judgment. Kennedy understood this. He also understood that
the responsibilities of human freedom grow in direct proportion
to human power. Exponential advances in technology, from

cloning to nuclear weaponry, place unprecedented moral responsibility on the shoulders of those who develop and control such technology. From genesis to apocalypse, powers once in God's domain lie now in our own. This is a spiritual burden, one Kennedy depicted in appropriately biblical language.

> Now the trumpet summons us again—not as a call to bear arms, though arms we need—not as a call to battle, though embattled we are—but a call to bear the burden of a long twilight struggle, year in and year out, "rejoicing in hope, patient in tribulation"—a struggle against the common enemies of man: tyranny, poverty, disease and war itself.

Throughout the Cold War, Americans struggled to balance the quest for freedom abroad and the preservation of freedom at home. The struggle against communism, however high principled, challenged the nation to define itself according to its own strengths, not merely in contrast to its enemies' failings. As the Vietnam War would soon demonstrate, the most ironic lesson of history is that we must choose our enemies carefully, for we will become like them. American civil religion is vital only to the extent that it calls the nation under judgment as readily as it calls it to arms.

Those who cringe at religious rhetoric in political discourse are right to point out how easily and often such rhetoric is abused. If patriotism is the last refuge of scoundrels, patriotism trussed up with God's mantle is potentially diabolical. The evils of Christian jingoism are on display throughout the nation's history. They assume an even more dangerous expression when employed to advance a state invested with nuclear capacity sufficient to destroy the entire planet. The glib coupling of nuclear holocaust with Christian Armageddon led to a bumper sticker popular in the late 1950s and early 1960s: "Kill them all, God will know His own."

If civil religion can be employed for immoral purposes, it

may also be so watered down as to have almost no spiritual content. But when true to the spirit of the founders, republican faith inspires a profound commitment to God-given liberty, justice with equality, the cultivation of dynamic pluralism, and moral responsibility. Bestowed with divine gifts, we are called under judgment. Epitomizing the moral eloquence of civil religion at its best, Kennedy closed his Inaugural Address with a reminder of this dual inheritance.

> Finally, whether you are citizens of America or citizens of the world, ask of us here the same high standards of strength and sacrifice which we ask of you. With a good conscience our only sure reward, with history the final judge of our deeds, let us go forth to lead the land we love, asking His blessing and His help, but knowing that here on earth God's work must truly be our own.

On November 22, 1963, Kennedy was struck down by an assassin's bullet. His legacy is one of spirit more than actual accomplishment. The 1950s cult of democracy was not redeemed by his stirring rhetoric into a public faith worthy of the nation's ideals. When the cult itself was broken in a paroxysm of civil rights and antiwar protests in the years that followed, the nation endured what might better be termed a time of "public faithlessness." But, sounding clearly almost half a century later, Kennedy's immortal words remain to remind us of the nation's purpose. They breathed new life into the American Creed.

11

THE AMERICAN DREAM

I have a dream that one day this nation will rise up
and live out the true meaning of its creed: "We hold
these truths to be self-evident: that all men are created
equal."

—Dr. Martin Luther King, Jr.,
August 28, 1963

TWO-THIRDS OF THE WAY THROUGH JOHN F. KENNEDY'S BRIEF
presidency, on September 22, 1962, thousands of people gathered outside the Lincoln Memorial in Washington to inaugurate
a yearlong commeration of the centennial of Abraham Lincoln's
Emancipation Proclamation. Governor Nelson Rockefeller
prayed that a Lincoln-like faith might arise to extend the full
reach of freedom to every American: "May God give us the love,
the courage, the understanding to see in perspective ourselves
and the times in which we live—and to make the faith that lies
behind this Proclamation truly live for all men in all places of
our land." Adlai Stevenson, the U.S. ambassador to the United
Nations, delivered the main address. Expanding the compass of
Rockefeller's prayer, he held up individual freedom as the "great
unfinished business of the world today." Rather than celebrate
Lincoln's moral accomplishment, Stevenson evoked his spirit.
He brought our nation under judgment. God may have created
all people equal, he said, but for many Americans equality of
opportunity remained an unfulfilled promise. Such self-criticism

would not weaken America in the eyes of the world, he argued. On the contrary, our defense of freedom abroad would become more persuasive "for being based not on illusions but upon the truth about ourselves."

One year later President John F. Kennedy proposed new civil rights legislation to Congress. "No one has been barred on account of his race from fighting for America," he said. "There are no 'white' and 'colored' signs on the foxholes and graveyards of battle. Surely, in 1963, one hundred years after emancipation, it should not be necessary for any American to demonstrate in the streets for opportunity to stop at a hotel, or to eat at a lunch counter." Such demonstrations did turn out to be necessary. Once again (to echo John Adams), the blood of martyrs became "the seed of the American congregation."

With Kennedy's assassination in Dallas that November, Lyndon Johnson received a national mandate to expand the scope of his predecessor's legislation and pressed successfully for its enactment. In his inaugural address, Johnson invoked the American Creed directly. "Conceived in justice, written in liberty, bound in union, it was meant one day to inspire the hope of all mankind; and it binds us still. If we keep its terms, we shall flourish." To this end the nation's spiritual progress rested— symbolically and in fact—on the witness and sacrifice of another apostle of E pluribus unum. Dr. Martin Luther King, Jr., followed in Abraham Lincoln's footsteps and gave his life that America might live up to its creed.

Raised in Atlanta, Georgia, in the household of a prominent Baptist minister, King conducted his brief life with prophetic urgency. As founder and president of the Southern Christian Leadership Conference (whose mission he advanced from the 1950s until his assassination in 1968), he was in the front line of almost every major battle for Negro equality. Inspired by the teachings of Mahatma Gandhi, Leo Tolstoy, Henry David Thoreau, and Jesus, he articulated a gospel of nonviolent resistance to evil, thereby both elevating and strengthening the power of his cause. From Montgomery, Alabama, in 1955 to Selma and

Birmingham nearly a decade later, King spearheaded a second American Revolution that, without his leadership, might easily have become a second Civil War. For his efforts, in 1964 he became the youngest person to win the Nobel Peace Prize.

At the time King's intrusion of religion into politics was rejected by some on the Christian right as anti-American and unbiblical. A young, prepoliticized Jerry Falwell condemned the ministers who marched with King in Selma in 1965. "Preachers are not called to be politicians but to be soul winners," Falwell said. "Nowhere are we commissioned to reform the externals. The gospel does not clean up the outside but rather regenerates the inside." On the left, African American spiritual leaders from Malcolm X to Adam Clayton Powell, Jr., lambasted King for everything from his dedication to nonviolence to his embrace of white colleagues to help shape the civil rights agenda. Resisting pressure from both sides, King marched onward with his "biracial army"—nonviolent, politically engaged, and spiritually charged—to redeem America.

I was one of several hundred thousand American citizens present outside the Lincoln Memorial on August 28, 1963, when King invoked a medley of American scripture to proclaim his dream. The entire occasion was charged with hope. King's March on Washington was the only mass protest ever to be covered live on national television, with his sermon simulcast on all three major networks. People thronged the mall, extending from the reflecting pool and Washington Monument to the foot of the Lincoln Memorial. Joan Baez, Odetta, and Bob Dylan sang. King's disciple and SCLC colleague John Lewis preached for the struggle to continue "until true freedom comes, until the revolution of 1776 is complete." King too turned the lectern into a pulpit. He opened by echoing Lincoln's Gettysburg Address: "Five score years ago, a great American, in whose symbolic shadow we stand, signed the Emancipation Proclamation." By Lincoln one major step had been taken toward the fulfillment of the nation's creed. The march continues, King proclaimed.

His most famous words, the ringing "I have a dream" peroration, were not in the written text. Moved by the spirit, he quoted several Hebrew prophets and then—looking forward to the day "when this nation will rise up and live out the true meaning of its creed"—King recited the words of a beloved American anthem. "This will be the day when all God's children will be able to sing with new meaning "My country 'tis of thee, sweet land of liberty, of thee I sing. Land where my fathers died, land of the pilgrims' pride, from every mountainside, let freedom ring." His most famous words every American should know by heart.

> When we let freedom ring, when we let it ring from every village and every hamlet, from every state and every city, we will be able to speed up that day when all God's children, black men and white men, Jews and Gentiles, Protestants and Catholics, will be able to join hands and sing in the words of that old Negro spiritual, "Free at last! Free at last! Thank God almighty, we are free at last!"

At the turn of the twentieth century, the civil rights pioneer W.E.B. Du Bois—whose death in Ghana was announced to the crowd on the day King delivered his address in Washington—described the experience of African Americans as a divided one, a "double-consciousness" caused by the denial of full freedom in the land of the free.

> The Negro is a sort of seventh son, born with a veil, and gifted with second-sight in this American world— a world which yields him no true self-consciousness, but only lets him see himself through the revelation of the other world. It is a peculiar sensation, this double-consciousness, the sense of always looking at one's self through the eyes of others, of measuring one's soul by the tape of a world that looks on in amused contempt and pity.

The substitution of tolerance for contempt and pity does not lighten the burden sufficiently to make the American dream accessible to African American and other minority citizens. In this respect, to follow the letter of new laws alone is insufficient for the realization of King's dream. Yet the dream is a simple one. It is the dream of all the world's religions, as expressed in each by a version of the Golden Rule. And it is the American dream, as drawn from our Declaration of Independence. This dream is predicated on the proposition that all are created equal, children of one God. Put the two dreams together and you come up with something even more precious, the Platinum Rule perhaps. Not simply "Do unto others as you would have them do unto you" but "Do unto others as God does unto you." Proffer them the same inalienable rights, the same equal standing, the same liberty that God has bestowed as your birthright. As expressed in the civil rights movement—and reprised in the campaigns for equal rights for women and homosexuals—when followed to its logical conclusion, such is the moral consequence of the American Creed.

King taught that the most promising path toward adjudicating human differences leads us to draw from common springs. In America, by tapping our nation's religious heritage, we draft healing inspiration from a universal source. This practice has international implications as well. Today the enforced reality of multiculturalism sponsors an unprecedented interfaith and interethnic dialogue. When multiculturalism is elevated into pluralism, its most persuasive participants almost effortlessly speak a common, if yet imperfectly spoken, language. The models here are many, including (together with King) those offered by some of the most universally respected leaders of the last century, each of whom brought or brings moral and religious intent to the resolution of political conflict. From Mahatma Gandhi to the Dalai Lama, Archbishop Desmond Tutu, Pope John Paul II, and the Vietnamese Buddhist Thich Nhat Hanh, the language of world peace and mutual kinship has been refashioned for a new age.

Each of these prophets offers a critique of the valueless nature of secular materialism while condemning the barbarism fostered by religious fanaticism. Each weds religion and politics while respecting the separation of church and state. And each condemns the purblind literalism that would yoke believers to the most incendiary texts in their respective traditions by invoking the saving and uniting spirit that distinguishes their own traditions' most luminous touchstones. "The greatest commandment is to love the Lord our God with all your heart, and the second is like unto it, to love your neighbors as yourself," Jesus taught. The Torah holds that "he who turns away from a stranger might as well turn away from the most high God." And the Qur'an echoes, "Allah put different peoples on this earth not that they might despise one another, but that they might come to know one another and cherish one another." More redemptively than global economics (which can divide the very people it interlinks) these universal religious teachings offer, in the language of the heart, a set of ideals that enjoins neighborliness and may therefore help to save us not only from our enemies but also from ourselves.

Diversity is a fact in American life, but pluralism is the ideal toward which we strive as a people. To put pluralism into practice requires more than mere tolerance. At one level to tolerate means "to bear with repugnance." Jesus doesn't ask us "to tolerate our neighbor as ourselves." He commands us to love our neighbor. The Declaration of Independence doesn't promote diversity; it inspires pluralism, which endows both freedom and diversity with moral content. "Whatever the name, some extrahuman Force labors to create a harmony out of the discords of the universe," Dr. King wrote. "There is a creative power that works to pull down mountains of evil and level hilltops of injustice. God still works through history His wonders to perform." More than any other twentieth-century American, Martin Luther King, Jr., by following the letter of the American Creed embodied its spirit.

The late 1960s were a tumultuous time in America. King was among distinguished company in opposing the nation's war in

Vietnam. Perhaps not since the Civil War had the nation been so passionately divided. Antiwar protesters turned the American flag upside down on their lapels (a nautical distress symbol that was read as an anti-American affront). Many Americans in fact did become anti-American during this period. Admittedly, the signals were confusing. When the premier of North Vietnam, Ho Chi Minh, had declared his nation's independence from France, he recited the American Creed.

> All men are created equal; they are endowed by their Creator with certain inalienable Rights; among these are Life, Liberty and the pursuit of Happiness.
>
> This immortal statement was made in the Declaration of Independence of the United States of America in 1776. In a broader sense, this means: All peoples on the earth are equal from birth, all the peoples have a right to live, to be happy and free.

To some patriotic Americans, in Vietnam we were warring against our own founding principles. Others, driven to reject everything that was American, adopted as their personal creed the writings of Mao Tse-tung. A third group supported the war as a struggle for freedom.

Vietnam and then Watergate left American institutions weakened, diminishing both the government's moral authority and America's self-image in the minds of a new generation of citizens. The climate of often appropriate self-criticism presented inviting opportunities for emboldened journalists; and historians, liberated from the constraints long established by consensus history, added documentary weight to the moral case against America.

But the era also witnessed significant progress, most notably in the campaign for women's equality. American feminists lifted their voices to advance the work begun in the nineteenth and early twentieth centuries by their suffragette forebears. They too were witnessing to truths enshrined in the American Creed. Some were explicit in making the connection. Even as civil rights demonstrators had conducted a sit-in at the Liberty Bell in 1965, feminists sponsored a notable protest for the Equal Rights Amendment in front of the Statue of Liberty in 1970. Though controversial at the time, most of the gains made by women in the 1970s are now embraced by a great majority of citizens.

By and large, American freedoms of speech and assembly were protected (or at least tolerated) during the decades of protest, and the goals sought by activists were partially and, in some cases, fully met. In many stirring ways, the years leading up to our nation's bicentennial were a magnificent exhibit to the world of democracy in action. Whether one's principal concern is civil rights, women's rights, gay rights, or the rights of any group in the population whose station is separate but unequal, the most persuasive argument for American reform (as has been true throughout the saga of our nation's moral development) remains the Declaration of Independence.

Yet, America seemed diminished—in the world's eyes and in its own—as the seventies came to a close. With lasting consequence, a steady barrage of corrective and therefore helpful exposés left the general impression that America herself was so evil that many morally motivated young people could not help but view their country as much worse than it actually was.

Perhaps the most ironic result of this period is that the end of the Cold War, with the fall of the Iron Curtain, was a more hollow victory for America (whose faith in freedom had been ratified) than it was for the people around the world who had been liberated from tyranny. As a nation, we appeared ambivalent about the freedoms for which others were fighting, freedoms inspired by our own experiment in democracy. How different this was from the end of World War II, when, contrasting ourselves and our nation to Hitler and Nazi Germany, Americans felt so superior that they became complacent and unself-critical. By 1991, when the Berlin Wall came down, we were so inured to our own wrongdoing that we had difficulty crediting ourselves and our system for a magnificent triumph of the principles on which the nation was founded.

Many Americans felt this irony deeply and resented it. However one may view his policies, President Ronald Reagan owed much of his electoral success and his persuasiveness as a leader to the eloquence with which he reclaimed American symbols such as the flag. When he spoke of the nation as a shining city on a hill, he recalled the dreams of our first European ancestors. His patriotic urgings were a tonic for national pride.

The country remained divided. For those to whom the American dream was a nightmare and the American Creed itself therefore abrogated, the president's flag waving was nothing more than camouflage for a bankrupt national ethic. Nonetheless, many of the things we take for granted in this country, especially our inheritance of freedom, people around the world long for with all their hearts. To celebrate the nation for its many blessings does not condone the distance we have yet to travel to reach that day when America lives up to its creed.

On April 12, 1968, eight days after Dr. King was assassinated (Lincoln too died during Easter week), Representative John Conyers of Michigan submitted legislation to establish his birthday as a national holiday. Two years later California had established a state holiday in King's name. Other states soon followed. But thirteen years went by before Congress passed Conyer's bill and President Reagan signed it into law. On January 20, 1986, Martin Luther King's birthday was finally celebrated nationwide, as it has been on the third Monday of January ever since. Given what it celebrates, the most recent of our national holidays is as true an American holiday as any that came before.

With Washington's and Lincoln's birthdays now celebrated together on Presidents' Day, King and Christopher Columbus are the only individuals to be honored with named American holidays. Martin Luther King Day is an emblematic American festival, hearkening back to the aspirations of our nation's founders. It permits us no easy celebrations, no mindless, instantly forgotten rituals, because the moment we pay attention, it reminds us of just how far we must still journey to fulfill the American dream.

12

"America the Beautiful"

What most needs fostering through the hundred years
to come, in all parts of the United States, north, south,
Mississippi Valley, and Atlantic and Pacific coasts, is
this fused and fervent identity of the individual, who-
ever he or she may be, and wherever the place, with
the idea and fact of AMERICAN totality, and what
is meant by the Flag, the stars and stripes.

—*Walt Whitman,*
"Democratic Vistas," 1882

Celebrations marking the Bicentennial of the Declaration
of Independence in 1976 were lavish and colorful, the marketplace flooded with red, white, and blue trinkets (made in China),
tall ships in New York Harbor, and fireworks galore. Otherwise,
little that was distinctive or memorable distinguished our two
hundredth birthday. Maybe we just weren't in the mood. In the
mid-1970s, with American citizens dispirited and divided following Vietnam and public cynicism toward government reach-
ing a new high in the wake of Watergate, the religious historian
Sydney E. Ahlstrom lamented, "The nation seems to be standing

between the times with no song to sing." A quarter century later, on September 11, 2001, America found its voice again.

The incineration of the World Trade Center transfixed a bewildered nation, drawing us into the world's violence and steeling our national will. The challenge was unmistakable and the afterimages almost unbearably poignant. A grieving nation witnessed countless deeds of heroism and as many reminders of our fundamental human kinship. As the soot and ash rained down, people—both literally and figuratively—became one color, class, and faith, carrying one another down stairs and falling to their knees in prayer. Ours was a single family, united as never before in recent history.

Not since Pearl Harbor had our nation witnessed anything like the surge of religiously charged patriotism that took place following the terrorist attack. One Episcopal bishop noted that, from diners to bait and ammo shops, signs reading "God Bless America" outnumbered those for "hot coffee." By December almost as many houses boasted flags as displayed Christmas lights. The Rockefeller Center Christmas tree in New York City was lit entirely in red, white, and blue; it looked like the top of the Empire State Building on the Fourth of July.

A less cynical nation perceived the need for and value of federal and city services and aid. Public trust in our government grew dramatically. Trust in one another grew as well. Repeated images of the horror were soon displaced by testimonials to heroism: firefighters rushing into buildings to help their fellows out; the courage of a little band of passengers on the doomed United flight 93, saving the nation's Capitol or White House from almost sure destruction; the heroic leadership of Rudolph Giuliani, a hitherto controversial New York City mayor who three months later was featured as *Time* magazine's Person of the Year. Above all, we witnessed the spontaneous splendor and goodness of ordinary citizens. Residents of the most cosmopolitan city in the world put aside all differences when called on for neighborly assistance. Where before so many of the images of America televised around the globe had advertised decadence, arrogance, selfishness, and criminality, the world at last was able to observe us as we like to see ourselves: a kindhearted and generous-spirited people.

Part of this makeover was the result of what is popularly known as the Buffalo snowstorm disaster scenario, when a common plight reduces everyday differences, of nature or opinion, to an afterthought. Yet, no matter how extraordinary the occasion, to view Americans of every religion and color demonstrating fidelity to their common humanity was nothing less than redemptive for a world in which divisions according to race, class, and creed are commonplace.

We also came together religiously. The memorial service at the National Cathedral featured Catholics and Protestants, Muslims and Jews. President George W. Bush took time out from attending to the defeat of the Taliban and the battle against Osama bin Laden to worship at an American mosque. Throughout the country countless citizens weighed their mortality and questioned their priorities, awakening once again to life's fragility and preciousness. We joined as one to mourn a common loss.

Most telling of all, where it might logically have been dashed following the attack by Islamic extremists, Americans of every faith expressed a deeper kinship with their Muslim neighbors. A Reuters poll taken two months after the attack registered a sharp rise in the percentage of Americans who viewed Muslim Americans in a favorable light. Before September 11, 45 percent of our citizens viewed their Muslim neighbor favorably; in November this gauge had risen to 59 percent. The change was most evident among Republicans, whose favorable opinion of Muslims soared from 29 to 64 percent. That the attested and observable rise in both patriotic and religious spirit following September 11 should also find expression in a commensurate growth in religious tolerance witnesses eloquently to the true nature of the American Creed—its ideal of a pluralistic union almost unimaginable beyond the borders of a society in which faith and freedom are honored equally.

Senator Hillary Rodham Clinton of New York had earlier modeled the way a nonfundamentalist might begin to bridge the divide. "The energy animating the responsible fundamentalist right has come from their sense of life getting away from us—

of meaning being lost and people being turned into . . . amoral decision-makers," she said. Admitting her sympathy for this concern, and thereby expressing an appreciation for the religious values of people with whom she might otherwise profoundly disagree, Senator Clinton struck a redemptive common chord.

Shortly after leaving office, President Bill Clinton demonstrated the same empathetic imagination in speaking about our neighbors around the globe. "Because we live in an interdependent world, we must accept the fact that all people are created equal, entitled to a chance at a decent life, that no one has a monopoly on truth, that we all do better when we help each other." Clinton summed up the faith of democratic pluralism in a single sentence: "One person's dignity is not by definition another person's humiliation; one person's work of God not by definition another's heresy."

At our national best, when we wave the American flag or affix red, white, and blue ribbons to our lapels, this is not merely an expression of patriotism uniting us against a common foe but rather an emblem of faith uniting us with one another. Our hymns of freedom are sung less in anger than in hope. It is these mythic overtones—not lost innocence or apocalyptic vengeance—that recall and then reconnect us to "the mystic chords of memory" of which Abraham Lincoln spoke. These mystic chords, which sounded clearly once again that unforgettable fall, contain the high notes of the American Creed.

In the weeks following September 11, among the commentaries distributed throughout the democracy of e-mail was an "Ode to America," written by a Romanian journalist. Cornel Nistorescu began by asking, "Why are Americans so united? They don't resemble one another even if you paint them. They speak all the languages of the world and form an astonishing mixture of civilizations. Some of them are nearly extinct, others are incompatible with one another, and in matters of religious beliefs, not even God can count how many they are." What captured the imagination and wonder of this observer were the many manifestations of public patriotism and piety. "On every occasion they started singing their traditional song, 'God Bless America,' " he observed. Reflecting on the first internationally broadcast charity concert, a star-studded, three-hour gala that took place five weeks after the attack and raised tens of millions of dollars for its victims, Nistorescu exclaimed, "The Americans' solidarity spirit turned them into a choir.

> I don't know how it happened that all this obsessive singing of America didn't sound croaky, nationalist, or ostentatious! It made you green with envy because you weren't able to sing for your country without running the risk of being considered chauvinist, ridiculous, or suspected of who-knows-what mean interests.

> Imperceptibly, with every word and musical note, the memory of some turned into a modern myth of tragic heroes. And with every phone call, millions and millions of dollars were put in a collection aimed at rewarding not a man or a family, but a spirit which nothing can buy.

At a juncture in our history when commentators rushed to declare irony passé, there is abundant irony here. For one thing, even as our self-appointed enemies caricature America as soulless ("the great infidel"), here an outside observer—one of many so moved—is staggered by overwhelming evidence of the nation's collective soul. For another, the choir of voices raised as one was raised most eloquently and often in singing not our stirring yet martial national anthem but "God Bless America," a hymn to peace, and "America the Beautiful," a reverent yet self-critical anthem written in part to correct our nation's course.

It could easily have been otherwise. After all, "The Star-Spangled Banner" took on new relevance after September 11, a relevance it had achieved only once before since it was written.

America was under direct attack, with bombs bursting in air over New York and Washington, D.C.

The first assault on Washington, near the end of the War of 1812, left the nation's capital in flames and First Lady Dolley Madison fleeing to safety, with the burning of the Capitol build-ing a symbolic affront that directly parallels the attack on the Pentagon 190 years later. Shortly thereafter, the government asked Francis Scott Key, a Baltimore lawyer, to negotiate the release of the physician William Beanes, a resident of nearby Upper Marlboro, whom the British had arraigned for "feigning friendship" during their retreat from Washington. Though Key accomplished his mission, he found himself temporarily detained on a British man-of-war. Onboard the enemy ship, and eyewit-ness to the shelling (with bottle rockets) of Fort McHenry in the Baltimore harbor through the night of September 13, 1814, Key awakened to marvel at the tattered flag still waving in the morn-ing light. His commemorative poem, "The Defense of Fort M'Henry," which ran the following week in the *Baltimore Patriot*, soon established its claim as our national anthem.

As with all our national hymns, "The Star-Spangled Banner" celebrates both freedom and faith, most expressively in the rarely sung and therefore little known final stanza:

> *Oh! thus be it ever when freemen shall stand*
> *   Between their loved home and the war's desolation!*
> *Blest with victory and peace, may the heaven-rescued land*
> *   Praise the Power that hath made and preserved us a*
> *   nation!*
> *Then conquer we must, for our cause it is just,*
> *And this be our motto: "In God is our trust!"*
> *And the star-spangled banner in triumph shall wave,*
> *O'er the land of the free and the home of the brave!*

"When our cause it is just" has rightly replaced the vaunting certitude of Key's original text, but the central motifs of the nation's mythos are nonetheless present here. From the outset of our experiment in democracy, America has known itself as both one nation under God and the land of the free. Though subject to unself-critical idolatry, each of these elements is central to the American Creed.

Every now and then some well-meaning group of citizens attempts to replace the "unsingable" and bellicose "Star-Spangled Banner" with "America the Beautiful." It took Congress two decades to make "The Star-Spangled Banner" our national anthem in the first place. The bill was submitted in 1912. After extensive lobbying by the Veterans of Foreign Wars, the legislation passed and was signed into law by Herbert Hoover in 1931.

But the controversy continues. "It is hopelessly out of date," goes the critics' refrain. Not to mention the fact that it is relegated mostly to ball games, where even professional singers break their voices on the high notes. The most recent failed attempt to legislate changing anthems was launched in 1989 by Representative Andrew Jacobs, from Indiana. "Passion is important in life, but to be steadfast is crucial," Jacobs argues. " 'America the Beautiful' is not boisterous. Neither is true patriotism, which is an abiding thing, calm and steady on stormy seas as well as in the safety of the harbor."

Representative Jacobs's sensibilities aside, the terrorist attack on America made Key's words relevant once again. For only the second time since it was written, its vivid language rang true. "The rockets' red glare, the bombs bursting in air, gave proof through the night that our flag was still there" actually matches direct American experience. Others, most notably (and, again, ironically) our old enemies the British, recognized this fact. Overcoming the scars of ancient memory, for the first time in history "The Star-Spangled Banner" was played at events sponsored by the British crown (at Buckingham Palace and St. Paul's Cathedral). Nonetheless, all across the United States during the weeks immediately following September 11, though it certainly was neither neglected nor forgotten, "The Star-Spangled Banner" was

spontaneously and almost universally displaced as our true national anthem by "America the Beautiful" and "God Bless America." I found its muted prominence particularly notable at
sporting events.

"America the Beautiful" may not be boisterous. And it certainly lacks the raw military chauvinism of "The Star-Spangled
Banner," but it is truer to the spirit of the American Creed,
uplifting reverence for liberty with a refrain sounding the values
to which our freedom is dedicated. An aspirational anthem,
"America the Beautiful" is reverent but not jingoistic. It ac-
knowledges the ambiguities of our history while challenging us
to recommit our lives to American ideals and fulfill the national
promise. It reminds us of the Pilgrims who beat a thoroughfare
for freedom across the wilderness. It beseeches God to mend our
every flaw. It invokes heroes who loved mercy more than life,
asking God to refine America's gold till all success be nobleness
and every gain divine. Elevating freedom by lifting the sights
of faith, "America the Beautiful" closes with an image of the
shining city on a hill that John Winthrop foresaw and Ronald
Reagan celebrated in his speeches:

> O beautiful for patriot dream
> That sees beyond the years
> Thine alabaster cities gleam
> Undimmed by human tears!
> America! America!
> God shed his grace on thee,
> And crown thy good with brotherhood
> From sea to shining sea!

How appropriate, at a time when the entire nation was brought
together in grief, that it was to these sacred verses we spontaneously turned, recalling ourselves to a victory of the spirit, not
a victory by might.

*   *   *

Katharine Lee Bates wrote "America the Beautiful" in 1893, inspired by the 360-degree view from the top of Pikes Peak in Colorado, where the Continental Divide parts the waters that flow from sea to shining sea. She had just visited the World's Exposition in Chicago and witnessed the "alabaster city" that shimmered like a dream vision on the shoreline of Lake Michigan. Traveling by train through Kansas on Independence Day—looking out at endless fields of golden wheat—Bates pledged in her diary to be "a better American for such a Fourth." She had already proved herself a good American, having threatened to resign her professorship at Wellesley College when the trustees proposed that all faculty sign a pledge swearing they were Christian. Bates called the request "intolerable." Shortly thereafter it was rescinded.

A minor published poet, Bates set her words for "America the Beautiful" to the tune of an equally unknown composer, Samuel A. Ward. Yet the combination of words and music is sheer magic. The folksinger Woody Guthrie, whose "This Land Is Your Land" also has achieved national iconic status, once said, "The main secret about singing ain't so much to have other folks listen as it is to pick up your own spirits." In the fall of 2001, millions of Americans picked up their spirits by singing Bates's lyrics as set to Ward's tune.

However sentimental its devotions may seem, the original lyric gives evidence of being, at least in part, a protest song. Writing in a period of high patriotism marked by a growing sense of American Manifest Destiny, Bates tempered her exultation of God's grace shed on America by urging the renewal of moral responsibility. As we have seen, the early 1890s were distinguished by a major diversion of American capital into the control of a handful of plutocrats who tapped the nation's vast natural resources to generate unprecedented wealth for themselves and their tiny class. "Till all success be nobleness and every gain divine" originally read "Till selfish gain no longer stain the banner of the free!"—a pointed reference to the danger economic empire building might pose to the American soul.

America's natural beauty led Bates to aspire to the day when "souls wax fair as earth and air." She rhymed the words *free* and *jubilee,* recalling the Liberty Bell and its biblical promise of debts being forgiven and the poorest unbowed by material burdens in the coming golden age of the Jubilee. If blunted, this spirit inspires "America the Beautiful" still in its more felicitous if somewhat homogenized form, underscoring that freedom is not only secured but also ratified and elevated by a faith worthy of those on whom freedom is bestowed. Reports are that soldiers spontaneously sang it on the announcement of peace ending World War I on November 11, 1918, a practice that continued in future Armistice (now Veterans') Day celebrations.

The other hymn to which the nation spontaneously turned in September 2001 was Irving Berlin's "God Bless America." Recast in 1938 from more militaristic material dating to the first Great War ("Make her victorious on land and foam"), "God Bless America" was conceived by its composer as a peace song. Berlin finished it at the end of October; Kate Smith performed it less than two weeks later during that year's national radio broadcast in celebration of Armistice Day. An immediate hit, "God Bless America" was so popular that the charitable foundation Berlin established from its royalties (the God Bless America Fund) vitalized the Boy Scouts and Girl Scouts of America for years. Though less explicitly moralistic than "America the Beautiful," by uniting faith and freedom in a similar manner, Berlin's peace hymn offers an equal contrast to the martial spirit of "The Star-Spangled Banner." Before asking for God's guidance "Thru the night with a light from above," "God Bless America" opens with a rarely performed proem:

> While the storm clouds gather far across the sea,
> Let us swear allegiance to a land that's free,
> Let us all be grateful for a land so fair,
> As we raise our voices in a solemn prayer.

President McKinley and members of Congress sang "The Battle Hymn of the Republic" after declaring war on Spain in 1898. But it was "God Bless America" that Congress turned to when they joined in song on the steps of the Capitol following the terrorist attack. "Civilization is always in need of being saved," wrote William James. "The nation blest above all nations is she in whom the civic genius of the people does the saving day by day." "God Bless America" and "America the Beautiful" emphasize not God's favor but God's guidance. They are not battle cries but solemn, prayerful hymns.

In his book A Religious History of the American People, Sydney Ahlstrom concludes that "the moral and spiritual development of the American people is one of the most intensely relevant subjects on the face of the earth." Despite our many flaws—which wealth and power magnify—the spiritual biography of America evidences remarkable moral growth. The lofty proposition of equality published in the American Creed notwithstanding, our founders tolerated slavery. In the Constitution voting rights were restricted to male landholders, with an African American male counted as three-fifths of a Caucasian male, and women not counted at all. Yet over succeeding generations (with respect not only to voting rights but to human rights in general) the letter of our laws has steadily approached the ideals expressed in the Declaration of Independence.

That we should turn almost as one to "God Bless America" and "America the Beautiful" at our time of trial is telling, given how eloquently these anthems capture the true spirit of the American Creed. The aspiration to "confirm success in nobleness" and "crown [our] good with brotherhood" has led succeeding generations of Americans to turn to God to "guide [us] thru the night with a light from above." One reason our religious history remains relevant is that the greatest legacy America offers—and the recurring object of our highest hopes as a redeemer nation—is not our devotion to freedom alone but the way in which, at our finest, faith elevates a freedom into a sacrament.

"What on earth can unite the Americans in such a way?"

Cornel Nistorescu asked. "Their land? Their galloping history? Their economic power? Money? I tried for hours to find an answer, humming songs and murmuring phrases which risk of sounding like commonplaces. I thought things over, but I reached only one conclusion: Only freedom can work such miracles."

Not freedom alone. What works such miracles is the union of freedom and faith. A freedom joining many distinct spiritual voices in one choir. A freedom inspiring a proud people to harmonize their differences into a symphony of millions, a symphony so powerful that Nistorescu was moved to call what he heard echoing across the waters "the heavy artillery of the American soul."

CONCLUSION

O, let America be America again—
The land that never has been yet—
And yet must be.

Langston Hughes,
"Let America Be America"

NOT LONG AGO, ROGER WILKINS, NEPHEW OF THE CIVIL RIGHTS leader Roy Wilkins and a professor of American history at George Mason University, visited the Jefferson Memorial. Standing beneath the dome of a monument dedicated to the memory of one of America's most honored slave owners, Wilkins brooded on Jefferson's complicity in his family's bondage. Then those immortal words recorded on a single slab of marble sang out their saving message. He could not help but marvel at "the throbbing phrases at the core of the American hymn to freedom that Jefferson composed and flung out against the sky."

Roger Wilkins is an American. Like all Americans, he participates in a yet-unfinished story. This story is both noble and tragic, but its genius is emblazoned from the beginning. "The Declaration of Independence," Wilkins concluded, "for all the ambiguity around it, constitutes the Big Bang in the physics of freedom and equality in America."

Unlike the Constitution, the Declaration is so explicit in its language that proponents of slavery finally had to reject it. In

1861, Vice President of the Confederate States of America Alexander Stephens conceded that the Declaration proclaims liberty and equality for all and that Jefferson himself believed slavery to be in violation of the laws of nature. Jefferson's ideas "were fundamentally wrong," Stephens proclaimed. "Our new government is founded upon exactly the opposite idea; its foundations are laid; its corner-stone rests, upon the great truth that the negro is not equal to the white man; that slavery, subordination to the superior race, is his natural and normal condition." Stephens once had quoted Proverbs 25:11 to Abraham Lincoln—"A word fitly spoken is like apples of gold in pictures of silver." Here is Lincoln's reply.

> The expression of that principle ["all men are created equal"] in our Declaration of Independence was the word "fitly spoken" which has proved an "apple of gold" to us. The Union and the Constitution are the picture of silver subsequently framed around it. The picture was made not to conceal or destroy the apple; but to adorn and preserve it. The picture was made for the apple, not the apple for the picture. So let us act, that neither picture nor apple shall ever be blurred, bruised or broken.

From the outset of the American experiment, our nation's leaders attempted to set a new mark. The meaning of our history sounds as clearly from the nobility of their ideals as it does in the incomplete fulfillment of their promise. To be a moral people is not to be a perfect people. (Otherwise there would be no such thing as morality, perfection stifling every effort to ensure its attainment.) But the founders saw to it that we would hold ourselves to a higher standard. "An almost chosen people," we demonstrate our greatness not by force of might or by virtue of our unquestioned economic dominance, but through rigorous moral endeavor, ever striving to remake ourselves in our own image. When we have approached true greatness, we have been great not because we were strong but because we were good.

In America the common good is grounded in a set of virtues—justice, liberty, and charity—that our founders established as touchstones of the good society. Devoted to the proposition that all people are created equal and endowed with certain inalienable rights, the American Creed combats tyranny while at the same time tempering the centrifugal forces of untrammeled freedom and relativism. The spiritual bond that protects religious liberty is our greatest achievement as a nation.

President George W. Bush (borrowing Chesterton's definition of America as "a nation with the soul of a church") summed up our union of faith and freedom to an assembly of students at Tsinghua University in Beijing, China, on February 22, 2002. "Faith points to a moral law beyond man's law and calls us to duties higher than material gain," he said. "Under our law, everyone stands equal. No one is above the law, and no one is beneath it. . . . Faith gives us a moral core and teaches us to hold ourselves to high standards, to love and to serve others and to live responsible lives." He coupled this paean to American faith with one to American freedom: "In a free society, diversity is not disorder. Debate is not strife. And dissent is not revolution. A free society trusts its citizens to seek greatness in themselves and their country." To a people for whom such thoughts are unfamiliar and to a new generation of Americans who may be unsure of their heritage, Bush introduced the guiding principles on which our nation was founded. He also acknowledged that the United States "has its share of problems, and we have our faults. . . . We're on a long journey toward achieving our own ideals of equality and justice. Nonetheless, there is a reason our nation shines as a beacon of hope and opportunity, a reason many throughout the world dream of coming to America." As so many of his predecessors had before him, Bush was reciting the American Creed.

The first American armed conflict of the twenty-first century is being cast by its aggressor in religious terms as a jihad against the infidel, with America blasphemed as "the great Satan." Osama bin Laden proclaimed that it was God who attacked the World Trade Center and the Pentagon. America is caricatured through much of the Muslim world as a godless society wedded to materialism and wanton in the exercise of its power around the globe. Yet this struggle, one that will continue into the indefinite future, is not between God and godlessness, but between competing theological worldviews, with diametrically opposed conceptions of the role religion should play in society to advance the greater good.

When religious believers confront neighbors who hold conflicting beliefs or don't believe in God at all, they have only four options. They can attempt to convert, destroy, ignore, or respect those who hold contrasting views. Fundamentalism embraces the first and, in its most radical expression, the second of these four options. It champions conversion but can sponsor destruction as well. Secularism occasionally opts for destruction (witness the crematoria and the gulags) but most widely embraces the third, ignoring religious differences as of negligible importance. The American way, charted by our forebears and codified in the nation's laws, represents the fourth path. In the spirit of liberal democracy—with respect given to the worth and dignity of every individual and minority rights protected insofar as the commonweal can still be maintained—religious pluralism is celebrated. America witnesses to a deeply held belief in freedom of faith, the rights of conscience, and the worth and dignity of every human being.

Some argue that all convictions are of equal value (except, perhaps, the conviction that all convictions are not of equal value). By this reading, there are no overarching stories or visions of the good life through which our lives acquire meaning. Yet it is precisely the vacuum created when we forget the nation's creed that invites occupation by the new fundamentalists. Our nation enshrines a radically different truth—an American vision, if you will—than that espoused by the tribalists who sponsor terror. If we lack the heart, faith, and courage to reclaim and model the "self-evident" truths on which our nation was established, we will remain vulnerable to those whose religious rhetoric fills the spiritual void we have left in abandoning the founders' creed.

Religion speaks in many voices, some uplifting, some incendiary. With its time-honored capacity to foster peace and its growing potential as an instrument for violence, religion is at once the most elevating and most dangerous power in today's world. The civil religious spirit too can promote self-delusion and national arrogance. Or—instructed by the American Creed and thus tapping the deepest sources of our common life—it can vitalize the nation, directing its might to secure the nation's integrity. When tuned to the highest anthems of our history, it offers a needful corrective to both relativist and fundamentalist pieties. Healthy expressions of civil religion mitigate the fragmentation of our national ethos, combat the moral attrition endemic to modernism, and secure the foundation of the common good.

The public and private elements of our religious identity as a people tend either to prosper or languish together. The chords of civil religion sound more eloquently when sectarian religious institutions are prophetic and strong. By the same token, when the values taught in churches and temples across the land reflect secular not spiritual values, our common faith is diminished.

Vibrant discrete communions and an overarching faith in American ideals are each important, but without fidelity to the latter the national center will not hold. In the midst of our revolution, Benjamin Franklin reminded his fellow signers of the Declaration of Independence, "We must all hang together, or most assuredly we will all hang separately." Franklin's rallying cry epitomizes the pragmatic advantages of *E pluribus unum*. *Pluribus* alone—the principle of sovereign individualism—endangers the health and vitality of a sovereign people. In our union of faith and freedom, neither alone could be half as redemptive as the two are together.

The evil deeds of our self-appointed enemies must not lull the nation into passive acquiescence to an end-justifies-the-means response. Since American union finds its noblest expression in the devotion we render to liberty, the right to dissent must be preciously guarded. From John Adams's Alien and Sedition Acts to the government's treatment of Japanese Americans in World War II and McCarthyism during the 1950s, history suggests that threats to security offer license to overturn fundamental human rights. The government has an obligation to protect public safety, but we must guard against politically convenient yet otherwise unnecessary abridgment of constitutional guarantees. Arthur M. Schlesinger, Jr., reminds us,

> When we talk of the American democratic faith, we must understand it in its true dimensions. It is not an impervious, final, and complacent orthodoxy, intolerant of deviation and dissent, fulfilled in flag salutes, oaths of allegiance, and hands over the heart. It is an ever-evolving philosophy, fulfilling its ideals through debate, self-criticism, protest, disrespect, and irreverence; a tradition in which all have rights of heterodoxy and opportunities for self-assertion. The Creed has been the means by which Americans have haltingly but persistently narrowed the gap between performance and principle. It is what all Americans should learn, because it is what binds all Americans together.

To remain true to its highest values, America must reembody the ideals of democratic pluralism, not rely on the vaunted superiority of modern secular materialism or trust in the persuasive power of military might. Terrorists may hate America as the incarnation of amoral secularism. But this caricature, if justified, is an America watered down. To survive the assault of neotribalism, America will have to revisit its shrines and recover its soul. American values go far deeper than untrammeled laissez faire capitalism and have nothing to do with materialism. They rest on the firm spiritual foundation on which our nation was established.

* * *

George Washington said in his First Inaugural Address that "No People can be bound to acknowledge and adore the invisible hand, which conducts the Affairs of men more than the People of the United States." The invisible hand to which he referred belonged to "the great Author of every private and public good." If America's critics are right, the true prophet, it would seem, was Adam Smith, who observed that the average citizen "neither intends to promote the public interest, nor knows how much he is promoting it. He intends only his own gain, and he is, in this, as in many other cases, led by an invisible hand to promote an end which was no part of his intention." Attesting to the influence of a very different invisible hand, Smith wrote these words in 1776, the very year Washington crossed the Delaware on the way to his rendezvous with American destiny.

Washington's Farewell Address was among the texts that Thomas Jefferson, apostle of religious liberty, established as required reading in his syllabus for the University of Virginia. In this speech Washington sums up the best of America.

Of all the dispositions and habits which lead to political prosperity, Religion and morality are indispensable supports. In vain would that man claim the tribute of Patriotism, who should labor to subvert these great Pillars of human happiness, these firmest props of the duties of Men and citizens. The mere Politician, equally with the pious man ought to respect and cherish them. A volume could not trace all their connections with public and private felicity. Let it simply be asked where is the security for property, for reputation, for life, if the sense of religious obligation desert the oaths, which are the instruments of investigation in Courts of Justice? And let us with caution indulge the supposition, that morality can be

maintained without religion. Whatever may be conceded to the influence of refined education on minds
of peculiar structure, reason and experience both for-
bid us to expect that National morality can prevail in
exclusion of religious principle.

Washington, who mentions Christ not once in the twenty
volumes of his collected papers, alludes here not to the saving
virtues of any specific dogma but to the highest attributes with
which we are endowed at birth by the Creator. Given how
lofty it was, he also wondered whether we could live up to our
own charge. Speaking of our newly minted experiment in democracy, Washington asked, "Can it be, that Providence has not
connected the preeminent felicity of a Nation with its virtue?
The experiment, at least, is recommended by every sentiment
which ennobles human Natures. Alas! is it rendered impossible
by its vices?"

Washington's questions answer themselves. They also remind
us of two aspects of our history that we flirt with forgetting.
Our nation is built on a foundation of belief, not on a foundation
of skepticism. And it is by our actions, not our words, that this
foundation of belief will be either justified or betrayed. To the
extent that the American people may be said to be chosen, we
are chosen to live up to our promise by acting according to our
faith.

"Observe good faith and justice toward all Nations," Washington beseeched in his closing words to a grateful people.

Cultivate peace and harmony with all. Religion and
morality enjoin this conduct; and can it be that good
policy does not equally enjoin it? It will be worthy
of a free, enlightened, and at no distant period, a great
Nation to give to mankind the magnanimous and too
novel example of a People always guided by an ex-
alted justice and benevolence. Who can doubt that in

the course of time and things the fruit of such a plan
would richly repay any temporary advantages which
might be lost by a steady adherence to it?

One saving grace of the American people is our optimism.
When transfigured by faith, this optimism is elevated to hope.
Hope's refrain is a dominant chord in the nation's history, present most tellingly at times of greatest trial. "I believe that we
are lost here in America," the novelist Thomas Wolfe wrote,
"but I believe we shall be found. . . . I think the true discovery
of America is before us. I think the true fulfillment of our spirit,
of our people, of our might and immortal land, is yet to come.
I think the true discovery of our own democracy is still before
us."

If the true discovery of our democracy is before us, to speed
that day's arrival we must revisit its sacred text. The American
Creed is a living will entrusted to succeeding generations by the
founders to advance the quest they began that witheringly hot
July two and a quarter centuries ago. If we follow in their footsteps and beyond, their dream for America will come true and
the grail of faith and freedom will be ours.

DEDICATION

(TO MY CHILDREN)

Dear Frank, Nina, Jacob, and Nathan,

The four of you and your friends represent America's future. My part will soon be played, and the stage of history will be yours. Yet I wonder how well I have prepared you for what lies ahead—and whether I have imparted to you just how much I love our country. How sad it would be, both for you and for your own children, if I failed to pass down the American tradition I received from my parents and grandparents. You will further shape that tradition in ways I can hardly imagine. But to do so faithfully, you must be conscious of what it is you are shaping. The word *tradition* traces to a Latin root that means "to hand over." From the same root we get the word *traitor*. I would be a traitor to America if I did not hand over our tradition to you in a way that might make it live in your hearts the way it lives in mine.

We take so many things for granted: our health, security,

sustenance, and the creature comforts we enjoy. In the United States we take our freedom for granted as well, forgetting how our ancestors labored to ensure it as our birthright. I'm not sure I've ever told you this: after love, freedom is the most precious of life's gifts. Freedom, and also faith.

American faith is one with American freedom. First religious and then civil liberty were the primary goals of our forebears. Having achieved these freedoms, they guaranteed them for us. Looking back over world history, we see that a relative few have been born truly free. And many have died in the struggle for liberty. To forget this fact is bad for our souls. It is bad for you, as America's children. And it is bad for the world, given how powerful our nation is.

You have often heard me criticize the policies of our government and the actions of our leaders. You have also heard others promote or defend America with words you find distasteful. You might conclude that, in today's world, America creates more problems than it solves. When we exercise our power wantonly, we *can* do great damage. But we also possess a history that instructs us in how to employ our influence and wealth. Ours is a good nation that sometimes does bad things. To be mindful of the latter and forget the former is both cynical and wrong.

Can you imagine how hard it would be to go through life with little memory of your past? How could you learn from your mistakes? And how would you know how you had arrived at your beliefs, or even what they were? This is why I ask you to listen to Thomas Jefferson. "*All people are created equal. They are endowed by their Creator with certain inalienable rights. Among these are life, liberty, and the pursuit of happiness. To secure these rights government is instituted among us.*" These propositions were unique in history when they were formulated in 1776 and remain unusual in the world even today. Ours is a proud heritage, not only a vainglorious one.

If you want to discover America, look in the mirror. Look closely and you will see your ancestors reflected in the cleft of your chin and the shape of your brow. Look more closely still;

imagine that you can see through your eyes into their eyes. You will witness many nationalities: English, Irish, Scottish, Welsh, German, and Polish. You will notice many faiths as well: Puritan, Quaker, Congregationalist, Unitarian, Methodist, Presbyterian, Episcopalian, Catholic, Mormon, and Jewish. You will observe a variety of occupations and conditions, and encounter as wide a range of convictions. And then look deeper, into each of their hearts. Imagine their dreams and their toils, their risks and their sacrifices.

Some of your forebears' prejudices and certain of their practices, such as slaveholding, will make you uncomfortable, and they should. Whenever we look into the mirror, unless we lack all conscience, we see things we don't like about ourselves. I am hopeful you will never disown your ancestors for their own mistakes but instead learn from them. They were flawed and complex individuals, just as you are.

Critique your forefathers and foremothers; try to understand them; forgive them; embrace them. But don't ever forget them, for you will be forgetting yourself. You are who you are not only because they chanced to couple and thereby kept the fragile thread that stretches from you to the beginning of time from being broken. You are who you are, in large measure, because they were who they were. So look in the mirror.

Frank and Nina, my children by birth, you are Richard Church of Plymouth. Seeking religious freedom, he came to America at the age of twenty-two in the company of Puritans who founded Boston in 1630. Richard moved to Plymouth and married Elizabeth Warren, who, at fourteen, followed her father to Plymouth three years after he arrived on the *Mayflower*. Active in civic affairs—several times serving as a judge in the "Grand Enquest" of both Plymouth and Duxbury, Massachusetts, where he moved in 1632—he was as a volunteer sergeant in the Pequot war of 1643. Richard was not the last of your ancestors to fight the Indians. Nor was he the first. In December 1620, three of your direct *Mayflower* ancestors (Richard Warren, John Tilly, and John Howland) were involved with Miles Standish in the first skirmish between the Pilgrims and the Pequots. Richard's life is barely noted in colonial records. But the ancestral line of Richard Church and Elizabeth Warren is vital to American history. Ulysses S. Grant traced his lineage to Richard and Elizabeth; so did Franklin Delano Roosevelt.

You are also William Worth of Nantucket. In the mid-seventeenth century, when he arrived there, Nantucket was part of Rhode Island, a colony founded to extend the compass of religious liberty to all people, not Puritans alone. William and his family planned to raise sheep in America, so they brought a number of breeding animals with them, together with their stock dogs. On its winter crossing from England, their ship was blown off course to the coast of Labrador. To stay alive, they were forced to eat not only their sheep but also several of their dogs. So grateful were they to their dogs that for generations the Worth family kept the surviving dogs' descendants, even after the family moved from Nantucket to North Carolina. Every Thanksgiving the Worths celebrated what they called the Feast of the Dogs. Repeating the family story, they offered up their thanks and treated their dogs with extra portions in honor of the animals own ancestors.

And you are William Clark. He served as a captain in the Revolutionary War, commanding a squad of sharpshooters. A Whig leader in Randolph County, North Carolina, William was best remembered for tracking down and killing two Tories who had murdered Henry Johnson, a leading local Patriot and William's neighbor. A decade after the war ended, William became a pacifist. His newfound Quaker faith also led him to become outspoken against slavery. In her notebook, at the turn of the twentieth century, Eunice Hadley Clark (wife of William's grandson Joseph), wrote, "He became so convinced that war was a hideous wrong that he put himself in an attitude to get a vision. Having become settled in his conviction that there was no Christ in either slavery or war, he pursued the only course open to him by joining the only Church that stood uncompromisingly opposed to both."

You are Ruth Lindley Hadley. Tracing their lineage back through the Plantaganets to English royalty, her family came to

America in 1712. As with most of the early women in your line, Ruth's labors were domestic ones and registered (implicitly yet eloquently) in genealogical tables more often than in civic record books. Not that her life was without drama. Ruth gave birth to Jacob, one of her many children, during the Battle of Eutaw Springs, South Carolina, in the Revolutionary War. In the heat of battle, she and Jacob were carried to safety in the woods. Ruth had fourteen children who reached adulthood. Each in turn married and raised ten children of his or her own. There were 140 first cousins who knew Ruth as their grand-mother. Her son Nathan maintained that she was proud of every one of them.

You are Thomas Hunter Barry and Margaret Ellen Ahern. Born in Rathcormac, Ireland, in 1830, Thomas immigrated to Boston at the age of eighteen and apprenticed as a baker. He married Margaret, another Irish Catholic immigrant, who was born on a farm near his home village. With their baby, Thomas and Margaret pioneered west. Traveling from Boston through the Isthmus of Panama, they set up residence at the Chinese Camp in Tuolumne County, California, where Thomas worked as a baker and merchant. Swept by gold fever, he followed the gold rush to Sonora, California, and then to Placerville, Idaho. Never quite striking it rich, Thomas and Margaret moved to Idaho City. The Olympia mine, named for one of their daughters, was known locally as Barry's Stairs, so steep and difficult was the road leading up to it. Thomas and Margaret educated their daughters at the Sisters of Holy Names Convent School. To earn a steady living, Thomas opened the Eagle Bakery in Idaho City, developing it into a general merchandise business, which he ran until his death in 1902.

You are David Burnett. Born in Scotland to the Burnet clan of Inverness Shire (adding a t to his name), he came to America in 1857. A Mormon convert, David settled for three years in New York City before traveling west to join Brigham Young and the Mormon community in Utah. Devoting his life to reli-gion, David returned to Aberdeen, Scotland, on a church-sponsored mission in 1883. He would have died there of a grave illness had it not been for a visit by the Mormon president,

Joseph L. Smith, who released him of his mission and brought him home. Shortly thereafter David moved to Franklin, Idaho, where he was ordained a high priest in the Church of Jesus Christ of Latter-day Saints in 1892. He left his children a long, handwritten ethical will, beseeching them to hold fast to the Mormon religion. Thanks to his phonetic spelling, as you read it you can hear his brogue ("farmerly, as farr bock as . . ."). David's will says nothing about the distribution of property but addresses only matters of faith. "There are great changes about to come to pass among men and nations to fulfill the Scriptures and the revelations given through Joseph Smith the Prophet, and you may not be prepared for them," he warned his children. "You will in a mishure be free from warr and truble that will aflict the nations by being here in the mountains, the place appointed by God for his people to flee to untill his Judgments aflict the nations, but that does not prepare you for the life to come."

You are your great-grandfather Chase Clark. After working as a lawyer in Mackay and Idaho Falls, Idaho, he followed his brother, Barzilla, first as mayor of Idaho Falls and then as governor of Idaho. A New Deal Democrat, Chase was assured of reelection in 1942 until he followed the counsel of Idaho religious leaders and pardoned a hundred prisoners to alleviate the severe overcrowding in the state's penitentiary. Two attended his funeral twenty-four years later. He lost the election by four hundred votes. President Franklin Roosevelt appointed Chase to the federal judgeship of Idaho, where he served until his death in 1966. Speaking as governor to a dinner meeting of the Committee for a Jewish Army of Stateless and Palestinian Jews in December 1942, Chase said, "An All-wise Providence deemed it best that the world should be made up of different races—of different creeds—and of different Nations. We, here in this great United States, are Americans, where all race and creed have been laid aside—where we have welded ourselves together under a form of Government that gives us all an equal opportunity—a people proud to fight under our own flag against the enemies of our American way of Life." Chase's favorite judicial act was the swearing-in ceremony for new American citizens. When he administered the oath, tears welled in his eyes.

You are your grandfather Frank Church. Inspired as a boy of fourteen by the career of Idaho's Republican Senator William F. Borah, he decided that he, too, would become a United States senator and chairman of the Senate Foreign Relations Committee. And he did. Frank (your namesake, Frank—the third Frank Forrester in our line of five) won the American Legion National Oratorical Contest in 1940. In World War II, Lieutenant Church served as an intelligence officer and was the youngest member of the officer staff at the U.S. Army Headquarters in Kunming. He accompanied the delegation that signed the papers of surrender in Japan. In 1948 (when your father was a baby), Frank was diagnosed with cancer and given six months to live. He beat the cancer, until it struck again thirty-five years later. Elected to the Senate in 1956 at the age of thirty-two, Frank served for twenty-four years. He gave the keynote address at the 1960 Democratic Convention, which nominated John F. Kennedy. Among the earliest Senate critics of the Vietnam War, he went on to lead important investigations of multinational corporations and our nation's intelligence services. He won four primaries in his race for the Democratic presidential nomination in 1976. Before his death in 1984, a 2.3 million–acre wilderness area in Idaho was renamed the Frank Church–River of No Return Wilderness Area in honor of his leadership in conservation.

This is but a small sampling of who you are. By my estimate (going back twelve generations), more than 150 of your direct ancestors lived and died in America. They run the gamut from Puritan ministers to Confederate governors. Some have marvelous names, like Ebenezer Clapp and Patience Little. These sketches also indicate only some of the Old World countries from which you came to America. Your great-grandmother Laura Bilderback (on your father's side) and great-grandfather Victor Furth (on your mother's) were of German stock. One Idaho ancestor, David Jones, immigrated to America in the mid-nineteenth century from Wales. Part of your mother's family came to America by way of El Salvador. The first church your father served as a minister was the very congregation that Richard Church worshiped at in Boston in 1630.

Jacob and Nathan, my children by marriage, your mirror too reflects America. All American mirrors do this, including those of your African American, Hispanic American, Asian American, and Native American friends. Every American is hyphenated, by the way—either that, or none are. Without this wealth of refracted heritages (from "old world" Africa and China to "new world" Haiti, Cuba, and the Dominican Republic), America would not be America. I am less familiar with your mirrors' varied reflections than I am with Nina's and Frank's, but those I do know add richness to my own heritage (a richness familiar to stepparents and adoptive parents alike).

Jacob and Nathan, you are your great-grandfather Harry Buck. Born Buchstein, at the age of nine he came to America in 1904 from a shtetl outside the Polish town of Grodno. Jewish boys as young as ten were being mustered into the Russian army and used for cannon fodder, so Harry's parents put him and his brothers one by one on the boat to America. Harry traveled by himself, first walking to the Baltic port of Gdansk. Exchanging all his money for a berth, he boarded a ship bound for Ellis Island. Upon arriving in America, Harry joined a cousin's family in Syracuse, New York, where he worked his way up from street sweeper to owner of the largest sanitation company in the city. Two of his sons (including your grandfather Earle) served in the American army during World War II. We have a newspaper picture of Harry in a crowd on the streets of Syracuse celebrating V-E Day in 1945. Harry brought the morning paper with him to your grandparents' house every Sunday when your mother was a girl. In order to encourage their desire for learning, he didn't want his grandchildren to know that he was illiterate.

And you are your grandmother Minna Rodnon Buck. Minna attended the University of Chicago and went on there to win her law degree. She was one of two women (the other was Congresswoman Patsy Mink of Hawaii) to graduate in her law school class. Five years later she had three young children, including your mother. Yet during the 1960s Minna helped lead several Great Society programs in Syracuse, including the Crusade for Opportunity and Onondaga County Legal Services. She went on to serve as counsel for the city of Syracuse and later for the state Democratic Party in Albany. Then she ran for office herself. The first woman and first Democrat to be elected family court judge in Syracuse, Minna served in that position for sixteen years, becoming one of the city's leading citizens. Since her retirement she has worked indefatigably for children's rights.

When each of you looks into the mirror, you will see many other reflections. But if you look carefully, you will surely see America. Note especially how the song lines of faith and freedom play throughout. What you discover in these reflections should do wonders in curing any latent cynicism. It may even inspire you to dream larger dreams.

Such inspiration may come from unexpected places. Let me tell you a little about an ancestor I discovered while doing research for this book. I alluded to her earlier. Her name is Eunice Hadley Clark. Eunice traveled west from Indiana as a young woman in 1882. She lived most of her life in Idaho Falls, Idaho, where her husband, Joseph, served as the first mayor. A Greek scholar and a member of the first class to graduate from Earlham College (a Quaker school in Indiana), Joseph was also a civil engineer. He proposed and designed a municipally owned water system in Idaho Falls.

I have been leafing through Eunice's scrapbooks. What I find there, in newspaper stories and in leaflets and clippings from magazines, is a portrait of the America we have lost and whose spirit we must somehow recover. Listen to the headlines of stories that caught her eye. "Prosperity and Conscience." "Washington Opposed Spiritual Tyranny." "Contest for President Proves Growth of Religious Tolerance." "Worship of Riches Assailed by Rabbi." "Pope Refuses Compromise in Film Battle." "Great Temple Built in Arizona Desert." "Gandhi Does Sewing Now by Machine." "Edison Believed 'Cross of Calvary' Was Greatest Monument of All Time." "Gandhi, Einstein Included

Among Greatest Men." "Idaho Falls Will Speed Work on Scenic
Area." "Nebraska Pen Becoming a Model Prison." And (my personal favorite) "Football Death Toll Is Heavy."

Eunice had a thing about football. She hated it. But, other
than that, every clipping she saved somehow feels all-American
to me. Note the liberal mix of religion and politics, of science
and theology, and, especially, the high moral tone (which today
we might dismiss as sentimental) expressed in everything that
caught her eye. There are sermons here by leading nineteenth-
century preachers from William Ellery Channing to W. W. Van
Dusen. She has a picture of a statue erected to the Rev. Henry
Ward Beecher and the text of a prayer delivered at the opening
session of Congress. There is a piece by Horace Mann titled "Be
Kind Boys" and lots of anonymous poems: "Know Thyself,"
"An Influence Never Dies," "This Is My Creed: To Do Some
Good." Eunice collected adages: "Liberty exists in proportion
to wholesome restraint"; "Religion is of the heart, not of the
head"; "Do unto others as if you were the others." And then
there are the stories about her family. Not only obituaries—
including those of children who predeceased her—but political
news generated by her husband and sons. Living with Eunice
Clark must have been a daily civics lesson. Certainly it worked.
Two of her sons (Chase and Barzilla) became governor of Idaho.
One of her grandsons (D. Worth Clark) was a New Deal U.S.
senator.

Eunice saved only one clipping about herself—perhaps there
was only one—an article from the local paper written when she
was eighty-seven. It calls her the "first lady" of Idaho Falls and
lists her many civic causes, noting that she "contributed her time
and effort to all the village improvement movements." The article closes as follows:

> Mrs. Clark recalls that in the early days here there
> were no class distinctions—the members of the three
> churches, Catholic, Baptist, and L.D.S. [Mormon],
> were the best of friends, and frequently held their
> socials together. Neighbors made a practice of calling

on one another, and strangers were given a hospitable welcome. At eighty-seven, Eunice Clark typifies the spirit of Christianity. Sympathetic and broadminded, she declares herself a non-sectarian, her quiet dignity crowning the richness of experience her life has given her.

My mother, Bethine Church, remembers her paternal grandmother as being always dressed in black or gray. When my mother was a little girl, Eunice told her that her favorite poem was something about there being "no sex in heaven." When people died they would take off all their clothes, swim together across the Jordan River, and come out spanking clean on Heaven's shore. Given how prim her grandmother seemed, this confused Bethine. Only later did she learn the poem's actual title: "There Are No Sects in Heaven." Eunice kept it in her scrapbook.

Eunice Clark was America. She embodied our union of faith and freedom. She lived the motto *E pluribus unum*. She was devoted to the American Creed.

After September 11, I find myself gazing into the mirror more deeply. I see the eyes of our ancestors looking back at me, their questioning, beseeching, expectant eyes. I will never write you an ethical will anything like David Burnett wrote for his own children. But I will fail you as a father, and my ancestors as a descendant, if I do not hand down the American tradition I inherited from our forebears. In that spirit, this book is my bequest to you (and to the members of your generation).

You will view our common history by your own light. And you will write your own changes on it. That is fine by me. It is the American way. But to be true to myself and to our American ancestors, before crossing the river to join Eunice, I must tell you our story. I offer it as a gift. It is the least that I can do. It may also be the best.

Lots of love,
Dad

ACKNOWLEDGMENTS

THIS BOOK EMERGED FROM THE CRUCIBLE OF 9/11. MY THANKS therefore go first to the people of New York City, especially the members of my congregation. Never have I witnessed so much love and courage. An act that was designed to divide America instead brought us together as a people. We saw our own tears in one another's eyes. The worst that human beings can do to one another evoked the best.

While gathering sermons for a 9/11 memorial book (*Restoring Faith: America's Religious Leaders Answer Terror with Hope*, Walker Books, November 2001), I found myself grappling with a set of broader questions. Who are we as Americans? And why are we this way? Does the first great conflict of the twenty-first century pit faith against freedom or two very different kinds of faith against each other?

At the same time I was putting the final touches on a theological memoir, which charts my midlife pilgrimage of faith (*Bringing God Home: A Traveler's Guide*, St. Martin's Press, March 2002). In length at least, the better part of my own journey is now behind me; by the same measure, my children's journeys lie ahead of them. What the future brings will depend in large part on what they and their generation bring to it. Without a sense of where they came from, how will they know where they are going, or why? I shared these thoughts with my editor, Tim Bent, a steadfast guide and inspiring collaborator. From our conversations this book came into being.

Inspiration also came from my colleagues at the Franklin and Eleanor Roosevelt Institute. By bringing one of its greatest chapters to life for me, Ambassador William vanden Heuval, Anna Eleanor Roosevelt, Arthur M. Schlesinger, Jr., and many others in the FERI family have invested my experience of American history with transformative moment. Bill is the most passionate citizen I know; Anne is my lifeline to her family; and Arthur, with moral urgency and inimitable grace, invests the nation's history with new meaning. I thank him for his attentive reading of my first draft, and also Christopher Breiseth, president of FERI, and Cynthia Koch, director of the Franklin Roosevelt Presidential Library at Hyde Park, New York, for their many helpful suggestions.

Others who read parts or all of the manuscript, saving me from even more mistakes than I have inevitably made, are my assistant Megan Martin, Kenneth Olliff (a doctoral candidate specializing in democracy and religion at Harvard), John Williams (a political economist at Melbourne University in Austrialia), David Blankenhorn (executive director of the Institute for American Values), and my All Souls historical mentor, Mary Ella Holst. My mother, Bethine Church, mother-in-law, Minna Buck, and brother-in-law, Michael Buck, offered encouragement and made helpful suggestions along the way. My research assistant, Adrien Smith, a sophomore at Wellesley College, was again invaluable in tying up loose ends. I also thank George Gibson, editor in chief of Walker Press, who kindly gave me permission to adapt here a few passages from my book *God and Other Famous Liberals* (Walker, 1996).

Above all, I thank my wife, Carolyn. For five months, she put up with crazy hours, cheering me on, cheering me up, and cheering my way. Words cannot express my wonderment and gratitude for her love.

Forrest Church
All Souls Unitarian Church, New York City
Memorial Day, 2002

Notes and Sources

CHAPTER 1: "A CITY ON A HILL"

1   "Behold I will do": Isaiah 43:19–20.

2   "It must never": Alexis de Tocqueville, *Democracy in America* (Everyman's Library, Knopf, 1994), II, 6.

2   "We speak with": *American State Papers and Related Documents on Freedom of Religion*, William Addison Blakely, ed. (Review and Herald Publishing Association, 1949), 305.

4   "In the name of God": *An American Primer*, 21.

4   "A democracy more": *Democracy in America*, I, 35.

6   "We must delight": *An American Primer*, 40.

7   "The city on a hill": Matthew 5:14.

7   "mere democracy": "A Negative View of Democracy," *The Annals of America*, I, 168.

7   "the liberty to that": *The American Puritans: Their Poetry and Prose* (Anchor/Doubleday, 1956), 92.

9   "We pledge to walk": Walter Herz, *Redeeming Time* (Skinner House, 1999), 6.

CHAPTER 2: SOUL FREEDOM

10   "All men may walk": *American State Papers*, 88.

11   "On the Lord's Day": William Warren Sweet, *Religion in Colonial America* (Cooper Square, 1965), 81.

12   "for the preservation of": *The Complete Writings of Roger Williams*, Perry Miller, ed. (Russell & Russell, 1963), VII, 268.

12   "Mr. Williams had declared": *American State Papers*, 87.

13   "a man godly and zealous": "Of Plymouth Plantation," *The Annals of America*, I, 81.

13   "I do affirm it to be": Martin E. Marty, *The One and the Many* (Harvard University Press, 1997), 37.

14   "the first person": *History of the United States, American State Papers*, 88.

15   "provide in their high wisdom": *The Complete Writings of Roger Williams*, VII, 183.

15   "lamentably be against": "The Hireling Ministry—None of Christ's," *The Annals of America*, I, 214.

16   "There is moral virtue": *The Complete Writings of Roger Williams*, IV, 365.

16   "no good Christian": *The Complete Writings of Roger Williams*, IV, 146.

17   "This assertion, confounding": *The Bloudy Tenent Yet More Bloudy*, Ibid.

17   "As formerly hath been": *American State Papers*, 51.

17   "For freedom of conscience": Ibid., 86.

CHAPTER 3: THE LIBERTY BELL

19   "Let the pulpit": Michael Novak, *On Two Wings* (Encounter Books, 2002), 49.

19   "Ring, ring": cf. Benson Bobrick, *Angel in the Whirlwind* (Penguin, 1997), 202.

20   "Proclaim liberty throughout": Leviticus 25:10.

22   "take away the Liberty": Winthrop S. Hudson, "Liberty, Both Civil and Religious," *The Lively Experiment Continued*, Jerald C. Brauer, ed. (Mercer, 1987), 77.

22   "heir unto by birthright": "English Liberties," *Nationalism and Religion in America*, Winthrop S. Hudson, ed. (Peter Smith, 1978), 198.

23   "the lengthened shadow": "Self-Reliance," David Hackett Fischer, *Albion's Seed* (Oxford University Press, 1989), 462.

24   "are not only under": Winthrop S. Hudson, *Nationalism and Religion in America*, xix.

24   "did not hesitate": *Angel in the Whirlwind*, 122.

25   "great revolutions were": Alan Heimert, *Religion and the American Mind* (Harvard, 1966), 291.

27   "A civil union": Ibid., 115.

27   "Every man being thus allowed": Kevin Phillips, *The Cousins' Wars* (Basic Books, 1999), 97.

CHAPTER 4: "WE HOLD THESE TRUTHS"

31   "Do the several": *The One and the Many*, 182.

31   "We hold these truths": *An American Primer*, 83.

31   "an expression of": Henry Steele Commager, *Jefferson, Nationalism, and the Enlightenment* (George Barziller, 1975), 81.

31   "the general effusion": Letter to Dr. James Mease, September 26, 1825.

32   "Indeed I tremble": *Notes on the State of Virginia* (University of North Carolina/Norton Library, 1972), 163.

32   "The sacred rights": "The Farmer Refuted" (1775), *American State Papers*, 123.

33   "We had no occasion": Letter to John Hambden Pleassants, April 19, 1824.

33   "Can we suppose": *Franklin: Writings* (Library of America, 1987), 61.

33   "that notorious atheist": Edmond Morris, *The Rise of Theodore Roosevelt* (Modern Library, 2001), 384.

33   "plain, pure, and unmixed": *The Age of Reason* (1794): *The Nation with the Soul of a Church*, 118.

33   "a grand errand": Winthrop S. Hudson, "Liberty, Both Civil and Religious," *Nationalism and Religion in America*, 82.

34   "a most ingenious": Merrill D. Peterson, *Thomas Jefferson and the New Nation* (Oxford University Press, 1970), 293.

34   "This is the age of experiments": Benjamin Franklin, *Autobiography*, 257.

34   "Interest alone is": Roger Wilkins, *Jefferson's Pillow* (Beacon, 2001), 62.

35   "Two things fill": *The Critique of Practical Reason* (1788).
       "that lordly ideal": Michael Harrington, *The Politics at God's Funeral* (Holt, Reinhart and Winston, 1983), 20.

35   "Great nature's law": *Sons of the Fathers*, 122.

35   "Men speak of": William O. Douglas, *The Mind and Faith of A. Powell Davies* (Doubleday, 1959), 134.

36   "The God who gave": *Jefferson: Writings* (Library of America, 1984), 122.

37   "Without liberty there": "Of the Mode of Education Proper to
      a Republic," William J. Bennett, *Our Sacred Honor* (Simon
      & Schuster, 1997), 412.
38   "twenty gods or": *Notes on the State of Virginia*, 152.
38   "No man shall": *The Annals of America*, III, 54.
39   "This right is": Ibid., III, 17.
39   "blackening . . . negrifying": Benjamin Franklin, *Autobiography*
      (Yale University Press, 1964), 214.
39   "How is it": Richard Brookhiser, *Founding Father* (Free Press,
      1996), 177.
40   "Nothing is more . . . be free": *Angel in the Whirlwind*, 359.
40   "incomprehensible". Jacob Needleman, *The American Soul*
      (Tarcher/Putnam, 2002), 260.
40   "cruel war against". Pauline Maier, *American Scripture* (Vintage,
      1998), 239.
40   "All men are": *The Annals of America*, II, 432.
41   "a day of deliverance": Andrew Burstein, *America's Jubilee* (Vintage, 2001), 136.
41   "to prepare sermons": *Sons of the Fathers*, 190.
41   "From the promulgation": Ibid.
42   "All honor to": *American Scripture*, 206.

CHAPTER 5: "A NEW BIRTH OF FREEDOM"

43   "Let us readopt": Garry Wills, *Inventing America*, xvi.
43   "Thomas Jefferson survives": Joseph J. Ellis, *The Passionate Sage*
      (Norton, 2001), 216.
44   "On our fiftieth": *Sons of the Fathers*, 192.
44   "holy purpose": *American Scripture*, 186.
44   "Can America be": Josiah Bent, *America's Jubilee*, 240.
44   "It may be": *Nationalism and Religion in America*, 73.
45   "The tree of": Edwin S. Gaustad, "On Jeffersonian Liberty,"
      The Lively Experiment Continued, 88.
45   "What, to the . . .": *The American Soul*, 241.
45   "There is no man": Ronald C. White, Jr., *Lincoln's Greatest
      Speech* (Simon & Schuster, 2002), 199.
46   "In the beauty": William J. Bennett, *The Book of Virtues* (Simon
      & Schuster, 1993), 798.

47   "Our progress in": William Lee Miller, *Lincoln's Virtues* (Alfred
          A. Knopf, 2002), 39.

47   "that sentiment in": Address in Independence Hall, Philadel-
          phia, February 22, 1861.

47   "If it can't": David Herbert Donald, *Lincoln* (Touchstone, 1995),
          277.

47   "Can the liberties": *Notes on the State of Virginia*, 163.

47   "a standard maxim": *The Annals of America*, IX, 23.

48   "He has made": Benjamin Barondess, ed., *Three Lincoln Master-
          pieces* (Education Foundation of West Virginia, 1954), 43.

48   "Ah Mr. President": Ibid., 44.

48   "Fourscore and seven": *An American Primer*, 435.

49   "In his words": cf. Robert Bellah, *Beyond Belief* (Harper & Row,
          1970), 178.

50   "since on the Fourth": *Lincoln*, 459.

50   "the legislation and": "Dred Scott v. Sanford," *The Annals of
          America*, VIII, 441–42.

50   "The perfect freedom": *Speeches and Letters of Abraham Lincoln,
          1832–1865* (Everyman's Library, 1910), 73.

51   "I care more": *The Annals of America*, IX, 30.

51   "I do not believe": Ibid., IX, 10.

52   "According to our": *Lincoln's Virtues*, 263.

52   "blowing out": *The Annals of America*, IX, 15.

52   "A house divided": *Lincoln: Selected Speeches and Writings* (Li-
          brary of America, 1992), 131.

52   "there is no reason": Garry Wills, *Lincoln at Gettysburg* (Touch-
          stone, 1992), 100.

53   "The more a man": A. Powell Davies, *America's Real Religion*
          (Beacon, 1949), 72.

53   "the great political": *Lincoln at Gettysburg*, 107.

54   "We deserve the": "The Christian Destiny of America," *The
          Annals of America*, VII, 109.

55   "with humble penitence": cf. Garry Wills, *Under God* (Simon
          & Schuster, 1990), 217.

55   "Men are not": *Lincoln's Greatest Speeches*, 197.

55   "It may seem strange": *An American Primer*, 442–44.

56   "We cannot escape": "Second Annual Message to Congress,"
          An American Primer, 426.

CHAPTER 6: E Pluribus Unum

57   "I'm glad to see": Donald W. Shriver, Jr., *An Ethic for Enemies* (Oxford University Press, 1995), 5.

58   "Quite half of": *Under God*, 211.

58   "We have, besides": *Lincoln at Gettysburg*, 86.

60   "Let us not": *Lincoln's Virtues*, 82.

60   "There are two": cf. William A. Clebsch, *From Sacred to Profane America* (Harper & Row, 1968), 215.

61   "Let the human mind": To John Quincy Adams (Nov. 13, 1816): Edwin S Gaustad, *Faith of Our Fathers* (Harper & Row, 1987), 88.

62   "this extreme tolerance": cf. *Sons of the Fathers*, xi.

62   "madmen, madwomen": *The Cousins' Wars*, 357–58.

63   "When, in the course": "Declaration of Sentiments," *An American Primer*, 378–79.

64   "children of the crucible": *The One and the Many*, 55.

64   "America is God's crucible": Diana L. Eck, *A New Religious America* (HarperCollins, 2001), 55.

65   "Men may change": Ibid., 58.

66   "Not like the brazen": *An American Primer*, 478.

67   "All the religions": "Democratic Vistas," *Specimen Days and Collect* (Dover, 1995), 220, 244.

CHAPTER 7: AMERICA'S MISSION

68   "Your mission is": Frederick Merk, *Manifest Destiny and Mission in American History* (Harvard University Press, 1995), 262–63.

69   "all women who": *Peacework Magazine* (May 1999), 17.

72   "Our fathers' God": *The Annals of America*, V, 554.

72   "I cherish the thought": Address on May 1, 1893: Lynn Sherr, *America the Beautiful* (PublicAffairs, 2001), 25.

72   "whether the American": Edmond Morris, *The Rise of Theodore Roosevelt* (The Modern Library, 2001), 473.

73   "The preservation of": Letter to Rev. Samuel Knox (1810), *Jefferson, Nationalism, and the Enlightenment*, 190.

73   "Our plea is not": Josiah Strong, *Our Country* (Baker and Taylor, 1875), 218.

74   "our rapidly increasing": Ibid., 165.

74   "the evangelization of the world": Margaret Leech, *In the Days of McKinley* (Harper and Brothers, 1959), 345.

75   "There are so many": *An American Primer*, 651.

76   "twentieth century crusade": Robert T. Handy, *A Christian America* (Oxford University Press, 1974), 130.

76   "I believe strictly": *The One and the Many*, 186.

76   "now openly": cf. Barbara W. Tuchman, *The Proud Tower* (Ballantine, 1994), 161.

77   "The twentieth century looms": Richard Hofstadter, *Social Darwinism in American Thought* (Beacon, 1992), 180.

78   "[You] will come away": "Going to Church," *The Book of Virtues*, 799.

79   "My country, right": "Anti-Imperialistic Conference Address," *Bartlett's Familiar Quotations* (Little, Brown, 1992), 510.

CHAPTER 8: AMERICAN FUNDAMENTS

80   "The sincere and candid": *Social Darwinism in American Thought*, 105.

81   "The idea of duty": cf. *The Politics at God's Funeral*, 117.

82   "destroyed and lost": "The Longing of Our Time for a World View," *The Weimar Republic Sourcebook*, Anton Kaes, Martin Jay, and Edward Dimendberg, eds. (University of California Press, 1994), 365.

84   "In the United States": Max Weber, *The Protestant Ethic and the Spirit of Capitalism* (Scribner, 1958), 182.

85   "We stand at Armageddon": *Nationalism and Religion in America*, xi.

85   "the tyranny of": Martin Walker, *Makers of the American Century* (Chatto & Windus, 2000), 12.

85   "fundamentally an ethical": Edmund Morris, *Theodore Rex* (Random House, 2001), 507.

86   "on a footing": *From Sacred to Profane America*, 164.

86   "the dangers of": *Our Country*, 150.

86   "God gave me": Alfred Kazin, "The Drama of Good and Evil
      in American Writing," An Almost Chosen People, Walter
      Nicgorski and Ronald Weber, eds. (University of Notre
      Dame Press, 1976), 55.

86   "a mammonistic organization": From Sacred to Profane America,
      275.

87   "a sort of magnified": A Christian America, 173.

87   "Saint Carnagie Temple": Samuel Hux: Richard S. Neuhaus,
      The Naked Public Square (Eardmans), 46.

87   "weaken the cause": Social Darwinism in American Thought, 200.

87   "Let it be understood": Ibid., 51.

88   "Man is the handiwork": Address delivered at the 1912 con-
      stitutional convention in Columbus, Ohio.

CHAPTER 9: THE FOUR FREEDOMS

90   "Just as our": The Annals of America, XVI, 42–45.

92   "That covers an": Samuel I. Rosenman, Working with Roosevelt
      (Harper & Brothers, 1952), 263–64.

93   "The business of": David M. Kennedy, Freedom from Fear (Ox-
      ford University Press, 1999), 33.

93   "The function of government": Arthur M. Schlesinger, Jr., The
      Cycles of American History (Houghton Mifflin/Mariner, 1999),
      239.

93   "must think of itself": Ibid., 239.

93   "The only thing to fear": First Inaugural Address, An America
      Primer, 864–68.

94   "With the clear": First Inaugural Address, Annals of America,
      XV, 208.

94   "The final term": The Annals of America, XV, 166.

95   "the great idealistic": Arthur M. Schlesinger, Jr., The Cycles of
      American History, 16.

96   "We are to be": Theodore M. Hesburgh, "American Aspira-
      tions and the Grounds of Hope," An Almost Chosen People,
      145.

96   "The stage is set": Address to Congress, July 10, 1919, A
      Christian America, 160.

96   "The so-called Christian": Ibid., 170.

96   "to establish a monopoly": Speech on the League of Nations, *An American Primer*, 816.

97   "Shall we join": Warren L. Vinz, *Pulpit Politics* (State University of New York Press, 1997), 51.

97   "the principle of justice": cf. Phyllis Lee Levin, *Edith and Woodrow* (Scribner, 2001), 203.

97   "the greatest hope": Roland Gammon, ed., *All Believers Are Brothers* (Doubleday, 1969), 236.

98   "The inherent dignity": *The Annals of America*, XVI, 514–16.

98   "It is my opinion": cf. Eleanor Roosevelt, *The Autobiography of Eleanor Roosevelt* (Da Capo Press, 1992), 322

98   "Denominations mean little": "Faith, Hope, and Charity, These Three," *All Believers Are Brothers*, 235.

99   "The Sermon on": *The Cycles of American History*, 71.

100   "Today we are faced": *The Public Papers and Addresses of Franklin D. Roosevelt, 1944–45* (Harper & Brothers, 1950), 615.

100   "In the past": *All Believers Are Brothers*, 238.

101   "It is high time": Ibid., 237.

CHAPTER 10: NEW FRONTIERS, OLD TRUTHS

102   "The rights of": *The American Primer*, 938.

102   "the cult of democracy": A. Powell Davies, *America's Real Religion* (Beacon Press, 1955), 77.

102   "I am the most": *The Nation with the Soul of a Church*, 25.

102   "Our government makes": *Beyond Belief*, 170.

103   "Recognition of the": *The Nation with the Soul of a Church*, 25.

103   "I believe that faith": "Crusade for Peace," *All Believers Are Brothers*, 3.

104   "the acquisition of": *The Annals of America*, XVIII, 1–5.

104   "Obviously something besides": Elmo Richardson and Chester J. Pach, *The Presidency of Dwight D. Eisenhower* (University Press of Kansas, 1991), 185.

104   "The conjunction of": *The Annals of America*, XVII, 3.

105   *under God*: *The Naked Public Square*, 76.

106   "We pray that": *The Annals of America*, 5.

107 "What seemed to me": *The Autobiography of Eleanor Roosevelt*, 438.

107 "now openly and": Theodore Sorensen, *Why I Am a Democrat* (Henry Holt, 1996), 33.

107 "Ask not what": *The American Primer*, 938–41.

109 "Kill them all": *Pulpit Politics*, 147.

CHAPTER 11: THE AMERICAN DREAM

111 "May God give": John Hope Franklin, "The Emancipation Proclamation," *An American Primer*, 433.

111 "great unfinished business". Ibid., 434.

112 "No one had barred": Ibid.

112 "Conceived in justice": *Beyond Belief*, 175.

113 "Preachers are not": "Ministers and Marchers," March 1965, *The Naked Public Square*, 10.

113 "Five score years ago": Taylor Branch, *Parting the Waters* (Touchstone, 1988), 880.

114 "The Negro is": *An American Dilemma*, II, 809.

115 "as God does unto you": Douglas V. Porpora, *Landscapes of the Soul* (Oxford University Press, 2001), 165.

116 "Whatever the name": *Tough Minds, Tender Hearts*, William O. Paulsell, ed. (Paulest Press, 1990), 3.

117 "All men are": Vietnamese Declaration of Independence (September 2, 1945): Robert Mann, *A Great Delusion* (Basic Books, 2001), 66.

CHAPTER 12: "AMERICA THE BEAUTIFUL":

120 "What most needs": "Democratic Vistas," in *Specimen Days and Collect*, 318.

120 "The Nation seems": *An Almost Chosen People*, 49.

121 "God Bless America": Bishop Hays Rockwell, *Restoring Faith*, Forrest Church, ed. (Walker, 2001), 3.

122 "The energy animating": cf. Martha Sherrill, "Hillary Clinton's Inner Politics," *The Washington Post*, May 6, 1993, D2.

1 2 3   "Because we live": Address, June 20, 2001, U.S. Air Force Museum in Dayton, Ohio.

1 2 3   "Why are Americans": *Evenimuntul Zilei* (Sept. 24, 2001).

1 2 5   "Oh! thus be it": Irvin Molotsky, *The Flag, the Poet, and the Song: The Story of the Star Spangled Banner* (Dutton, Penguin Group, 2001).

1 2 6   "Passion is important": "The Anthem Under Fire," *The Washington Post*, December 7, 1989, A26.

1 2 7   "O beautiful for": *The Annals of America*, XII, 1.

1 2 8   "A better American": *America the Beautiful*, 29.

1 2 8   "The main secret": cf. Colman McCarthy, *The Washington Post* December 16, 1989, A31.

1 2 8   "Till selfish gain": *America the Beautiful*, 57.

1 2 9   "While the storm": *The Annals of America*, XV, 525.

1 3 0   "Civilization is always": *Memoirs and Studies* (1911), cf. George F. Will, *Statecraft as Soulcraft* (Simon and Schuster, 1983), 161.

1 3 0   "the moral and": *A Religious History of the American People* (Yale University Press, 1972), xii.

Conclusion

1 3 2   "O, let America": *The Collected Poems of Langston Hughes* (Alfred A. Knopf, 2001), 189.

1 3 2   "the throbbing phrases": *Jefferson's Pillow*, 2.

1 3 2   "The Declaration of": Ibid., 140.

1 3 3   "were fundamentally wrong": *Lincoln's Virtues*, 433.

1 3 3   "The expression of": Ibid.

1 3 4   "a nation with": *The New York Times*, February 22, 2002, A1.

1 3 6   "We must all hang together": Esmond Wright, *Franklin of Philadelphia* (Belknap Press, Harvard University, 1991), 247.

1 3 7   "When we talk": Arthur M. Schlesinger, Jr., *The Disuniting of America* (Norton, 1992), 136.

1 3 8   "No people can": *An American Primer*, 192.

1 3 8   "neither intends to": *The Wealth of Nations*, IV, 2.

1 3 8   "Of all the dispositions": *An American Primer*, 221–22.

1 4 0   "I believe that we are lost,": *You Can't Go Home Again* (Perennial Classics, 1998), 741.

The Reverend Forrest Church is serving in his twenty-fifth year as senior minister of All Souls Unitarian Church in New York City. Educated at Stanford University, Harvard Divinity School, and Harvard University (where he received his Ph.D. in church history in 1978), he has written or edited twenty books, including *The Jefferson Bible, Restoring Faith: America's Religious Leaders Answer Terror with Hope,* and *Bringing God Home: A Traveler's Guide.*